WHAT A MAN WEIGHS

Sherry Kramer

BROADWAY PLAY PUBLISHING INC
224 E 62nd St, NY, NY 10065
www.broadwayplaypub.com
info@broadwayplaypub.com

WHAT A MAN WEIGHS
© Copyright 1993 Sherry Kramer

First printing as an acting edition: January 1993
First printing, this trade edition: December 2010
I S B N: 978-0-88145-440-6

Book design: Marie Donovan
Word processing: Microsoft Word for Windows
Typographic controls: Xerox Ventura Publisher 2.0 P E
Typeface: Palatino
Printed and bound in the U S A

WHAT A MAN WEIGHS had its first performance
at the Second Stage Theater, New York City (Robyn
Goodman and Carole Rothman, Artistic Directors) on
25 April 1990. The cast and creative contributors were:

JOAN..Christine Estabrook
RUTH.. Harriet Harris
THE DEBBIE .... Katherine Hiler
HASELTINE ....Richard Cox

Director...Carole Rothman
Set design.. Andrew Jackness
Lighting design ....Dennis Parichy
Costume design... Susan Hilferty
Sound design................................... Gary & Timmy Harris
Hair design...Antonio Soddu
Stage manager.......................................Pamela Eddington

CHARACTERS

JOAN— She is thirty-five. That age when the young truths stop making sense. JOAN has a great love of heights. If this were a different play, she might be a mountain climber or a balloonist...but since it isn't, she's a book conservationist. A good one.

RUTH— She has been JOAN's best friend since college. RUTH needs a great love of heights like she needs a hole in her head. If this were another play...well, anyway, she's also a book conservationist. She's good at what she does, too, but she has to work longer and harder at it.

HASELTINE— (Pronounced Haz-el-teen, stress on the Has) He is around forty—no one happens to ask him his age in this play, but if they did, he'd probably lie about it. He is a man who never apologizes: Does the lion send a condolence card to the family of the antelope? No. He does what he does because he has to. It's his nature. He's not conventionally handsome. Instead, he has the kind of charisma that makes every woman he meets believe she is the only woman in the world who is aware of his devastating, secret attractiveness. Not a snake...not a sleaze...he's a man with a great big heart. And a great big hard-on.

THE DEBBIE. She is sometimes nineteen, sometimes thirty-five. She probably should be played by one of those forty year-old actresses who often pass for fifteen.

SETTING

A tall staircase rises up as high as it can go. It branches off, a few feet above the floor, into two other staircases. These lead to two major areas—JOAN's apartment, and a multipurpose landing. If fly space permits, there can be other small landings, placed higher up the staircase. At the bottom of the staircase, wrapped around it or to one side, is the book conservation lab of a large university. The lab is a basement room—conservation labs are almost always given the least desirable spaces available in a library. The space is small, functional, and filled with books and artifacts in various stages of repair, plus work tables, large, almost medieval-looking equipment, and racks of simple, elegant tools. Very orderly. Clearly a place where things are made by hand, where people work side by side, and love what they do.

On one wall of the lab, a large, beautifully handmade dart board. This is not a regulation size board—it's at least twice normal size. The numbers in the sections of the board are elaborate, done like those capital letters at the beginnings of paragraphs in illuminated manuscripts.

Most important feature of the dart board—the sound the darts make when they hit is a loud, clear punctuation.

In many ways, the entire play takes place on the staircase. A set that places too much weight on the realistic representation of objects will not serve the play.

He who makes a beast of himself, gets rid of the pain of being a man.
Samuel Johnson

PROLOGUE

JOAN: (*In spot, as she places her foot on the first step of the tallest set of stairs—or perhaps the first words are said in darkness, before the spot hits her, already in position.*) I climb the stairs. (*She begins to climb.*) I climb the stairs, and I think—oh yes, he'll be there, he'll be there, and I'll walk through him into another world, and none of the things that make me frightened will ever touch me again, and everything that was ever ugly about me will drop away from me like water. I will be free of it all. I want to fall down on my knees, I am so goddamn grateful, as I climb the stairs, at the thought of being free, and so I do, in my mind, I fall down on my knees in my mind as I climb the stairs. He is there, and he has freed me from ugliness forever, from the lines around my eyes, the folds beneath my breasts, he has freed me from my thighs, he has freed me from it all. And the longing bucks inside me, and the heat has just kicked in, and I am climbing the stairs, and I am on my knees, and I am so goddamn beautiful, but it's the heat, in the end, that makes me know. That this is true.

Everything else could betray me. Everything else I could just kick aside. But not that heat. That heat doesn't lie, it has never lied, it is my truth, my own, and it does not lie. (*She is at the very top of the stairs, past the landings leading anywhere.*) I have climbed the stairs. And I am filled with him. (*She faces the audience.*)

I love this daydream.

And I hate myself for dreaming it.
I have climbed the stairs. And I am filled with him.
And he isn't there.

(*Blackout*)

END OF PROLOGUE

ACT ONE

Scene One

(The workshop of the book conservation department. It is night, late at night. Work on the worktables is covered with large white pieces of paper, which are called blotters.)

(RUTH is at her workbench, firmly and delicately removing something that has been glued to an old manuscript. She pulls slowly, and evenly, almost too slowly to stand.)

(JOAN is sitting on another high stool next to RUTH. She has a dart in her hand.)

RUTH: *(Sighing)* Men.

JOAN: *(Letting the dart fly at the dart board)* Men.

RUTH: You can't live with 'em—

JOAN: And you can't get 'em to dress up in a skimpy cocktail dress, and dance the watusi no matter what you promise them, and no matter how hard you try. *(She cocks her head to one side.)* But why did we want them to? Why was it so important?

RUTH: God, we were stoned—we called up half the boys in the senior class, none of them would come over, so we decided to put on the skimpy dresses ourselves. I struggled into this lemon chiffon monstrosity, and you had dug up this red beaded spaghetti strap thing, but you wouldn't get dressed, you just stood there, staring at that red dress, and

finally I came in and you were on your knees, with that
dress spread out on the floor in front of you, and you
were weeping, and no matter what I said to you, the
only thing you would say was, "The part of my brain
that puts the dress on is gone. It's gone. It's gone. It's
gone."

JOAN: No.

RUTH: No what.

JOAN: No, I don't remember that.

RUTH: Come on—

JOAN: That's wasn't me.

RUTH: It was too.

JOAN: No, it wasn't, it was Claudia Bently.

RUTH: *Shit!*

JOAN: Shit. (*And lets a dart fly. As always, it is not
important where on the dart board the dart actually lands—
there is a Zenness about the act of the throw, and the sound,
that is all that matters.*)

RUTH: It wasn't you. It was Claudia Bently. *Shit!*
wonder where she is now.

JOAN: Whidbey Island, Washington. Mother of three.
All have her hideous feet and their father's vacant
stare. (*She says fast, canted, snapped:*) Happiness.
Happiness. Happiness. (*And lets the dart fly. She cocks
her head to one side.*) I'm working on that one. Tricky
bastard.

RUTH: I'm still working on how I got you and Claudia
Bently confused. Don't you think that's a little funny?

JOAN: Not really. A very little funny, I suppose. When
you consider that Claudia looks like a ferret, talks like
a duck, and has the brains of a trout raised on a fish
farm. A very little funny—but not much, no.

RUTH: I get sick whenever I think of her. Just sick. Why should she be the one who's happy? Why, of the three of us, should she be the one who landed the perfect man?

JOAN: You think Rick's perfect?

RUTH: No, but she does.

JOAN: Well, that's why she's happy. (*She hands* RUTH *a dart.*) Men.

RUTH: (*Throwing the dart*) Men. Thank you. That helped put it all in perspective. We are all the authors of our happiness, is that it? Then how come I seem to have written mine in invisible ink?

JOAN: No such thing as invisible ink, Ruth. Rule number one:

RUTH/JOAN: Nothing you do to paper ever goes away.

JOAN: (*She picks up a stiff piece of paper that has been soaking in a bath.*) Especially if it's been laminated.

RUTH: Don't take it so personally. Some bubble-headed conservator did not laminate that document thirty years ago just to torture you.

JOAN: How do you know?

RUTH: Look, Joan, if you didn't want to work on that project, why did you ask for it?

JOAN: I didn't ask for it.

RUTH: You did so. You always ask for the basket cases.

JOAN: Well, someone has to do them.

RUTH: Good point. Excellent point. All hail Saint Joan of the Bookmark, the Mother Teresa of the ripped, torn, and laminated.

(JOAN *places a blotter over the Yeats letter, turns to go.*)

RUTH: Where you going?

JOAN: Home. It's late. You ready?

RUTH: Well, not quite.

JOAN: What do you mean, not quite. How long does it take to unbind something, five minutes?

RUTH: More or less.

JOAN: So what's the problem?

RUTH: Rebinding takes a few minutes more...

JOAN: Ruth! We'll be here all night!

RUTH: You know I have to have this ready next week! I'm not as fast as you are. I have to be able to take my time—

JOAN: But it's a simple project.

RUTH: Not for me.

JOAN: What are you talking about, you're the best when it comes to this kind of work. Haseltine said so himself.

RUTH: He told you that? He really did? He really said I was the best?

JOAN: Yeah.

RUTH: When?

JOAN: I don't remember exactly, Ruth.

RUTH: He really said I was the best?

JOAN: Jesus Christ, no, of course he didn't say it. I made it up. You found me out. Of course your boss would never compliment you on your work. Of course he wouldn't say you were the best.

RUTH: Well, I'm not. I'm good—at some things, yes. But Haseltine is the best. You said so yourself.

JOAN: I never said he was the best. I said he was possessed.

RUTH: Well, so was Walt Whitman. Look at this. (*She continues working, showing* JOAN *as she goes.*) Safety pins. The man made his revisions and pinned them to the manuscript with safety pins. They're covered with rust. It's eating though the paper. The essential question is, what's more important—the paper, or the rust. To get rid of the rust, I have to get rid of the pins. And they're historical pins. Historical safety pins. Which makes the rust historical—or does it? I'm beginning to have dreams about rust. Ashes to ashes, rust to rust. They used to believe rust was an animal, did you know that?

JOAN: It is an animal. Just a very small one.

RUTH: And with a small regard for the works of Walt Whitman. And then there's the glue. What he didn't pin to it, he glued over. God, what they used to use for paste. I don't know what to do. Half the time I'm so sure—the integrity of the manuscript comes first, preserve it for future generations, fuck the rust. And then the rest of the time I—I don't know. You get so hung up on doing something wrong, you can't do anything. You get so scared if you end up doing it right it's just an accident.

JOAN: Why do you say things like that?

RUTH: Like what?

JOAN: Like you don't know what you're doing?

RUTH: Of course I know what I'm doing.

JOAN: Then why do you say things like that?

RUTH: You say things like that.

JOAN: I do not.

RUTH: You do so.

JOAN: Well, I don't mean them.

RUTH: Then why do you say them?

JOAN: Look, Ruth, all I'm saying is, when you do something right, it's not an accident. Not at work, anyway. When you do something right at work, it's because you're good at what you do. Now in life, of course, it's a different story. In life nothing happens because you're good. Happiness itself, for instance, is something that just happens to you, period. Just like an accident.

RUTH: You never had an accident.

JOAN: Not here in the lab, but I've had them in life.

RUTH: You have not.

JOAN: What do you call Mark? (*Dart*) What do you call Larry? (*Dart*) What do you call—

RUTH: Not the same thing. Not at all.

JOAN: Accidents should happen to you when you're young. They're part of the adventure, they mold you, change you. All they do is make you wish you were young, when they happen to you when you're old.

RUTH: You don't know the first thing about accidents. You never had one.

JOAN: Well, that's not my fault, is it? A time comes in a woman's life when she needs to use the metaphor of an accident. Is it her fault she's never had a bona fide accident? Even the accident of happiness? (*Fast, as before, but anger there too*) Happiness. Happiness. Happiness. (*Dart*) What the hell. It's too late for me to have an accident. I mean, I don't even have somebody's name to call out, you know? And you do need a man's name to call out. You do. Even if you're just imagining an accident. I don't have one goddamn name to call out in a dramatic operating room sequence where I bleed out, start to die, call out his name with my last breath, and then miraculously return to life.

RUTH: Do you carry a purse?

JOAN: What?

RUTH: Do you carry a purse?

JOAN: Of course I do, you know I carry a purse.

RUTH: Then you're all set. You don't need a man to call out for—all you need is your purse.

JOAN: What are you talking about?

RUTH: Remember when I had my accident?

JOAN: Of course.

RUTH: Well, I didn't call out for a man when I came to. The first thing I asked for was my purse. They told me in the hospital that's the first thing a woman always says after an accident. "Where's my purse."

JOAN: That's very interesting.

RUTH: I thought so.

JOAN: You know what the last thing they say men in plane crashes say?

RUTH: What?

JOAN: They say "shit". (*She throws a dart.*)

RUTH: How do they know?

JOAN: From black boxes, you know, that they recover from the wreck. Shit is almost always the last thing the pilots say. Oh, except that time in San Diego, remember that? I always cry when I think of it. They've got two seconds left, they all know they're going down, and some guy in the cockpit calls out, "Ma, I love you." It always makes me cry.

RUTH: You're not crying now.

JOAN: No, I don't cry anymore. Even for things that always make me cry.

RUTH: If you had an accident, you could call out for your mother.

JOAN: Are you kidding? No way. A man calling out for his mother is one thing. But a grown woman calling out to hers?

RUTH: Yeah. You're much better off sticking with your purse.

JOAN: On the operating table? I'm going to call out for my purse on the table, Ruth? No, Ruth, I don't think so. Some rules are made. They are set in stone. Men call out for their mothers. But a woman cries out for—

RUTH/JOAN: —her man. (JOAN *lets a dart fly on "man".*)

(*Lights down on lab area.*)

Scene Two

(*Lights up on* THE DEBBIE *and* HASELTINE, *standing in the doorway on a landing, midway up the stairs.*)

(THE DEBBIE *is wearing a slip. She is somewhat in disarray. She is screaming at* HASELTINE, *who is less than half-dressed, hitching up his pants, as he stumbles out of her apartment, trying to shield himself from his shoes, which* THE DEBBIE *is throwing at him, as well as his shirt, jacket, and cap.*)

(*We hear the first line of this scene immediately after the last line of Scene One.*)

THE DEBBIE: *You son of a bitch! You goddamn fucking son of a bitch! I ever see you again, I'll scratch your eyes out, you hear me! You ever see me again, you run! I ever get you within range again, I'm biting it off. You hear me! I'm biting the damn thing off!* (*She slams the door.*)

(HASELTINE *walks down the steps, and gets dressed the rest of the way. He ties his tie, and shifts his jacket squarely on his shoulders. He sits down on the bottom step, puts his socks on, then one shoe. He starts to put the other shoe on.*)

(*He holds a woman's shoe up to the light—a dark pump, something that might have passed, in the moment of* THE DEBBIE'*s rage, for his shoe, but now is definitely not. He considers it all grimly.*)

(*He gets up, one shoe off, one shoe on, and climbs the stairway to her door. He knocks.*)

(THE DEBBIE *opens the door, and wraps her arms around him, sobbing.* HASELTINE *doesn't return the embrace.*)

THE DEBBIE: Thank God you came back. Thank God. I didn't mean it. I didn't mean it. I—

(HASELTINE *gently, firmly pushes* THE DEBBIE *away from him. He holds out the shoe. She backs away from him a step.*)

THE DEBBIE: Why?

(HASELTINE *shrugs.*)

THE DEBBIE: Why is it like this? It wasn't like this in the beginning. It wasn't like this at all. I try to hang on to it. I try—

HASELTINE: Debbie, please. Debbie, listen to me Debbie. I have to go. (*He holds out the shoe again.*)

THE DEBBIE: (*She nods, and disappears. She returns after a moment with his shoe.*) Help me. Please—I know I can't—I know you don't—I know you don't love me. I know that. But I can't believe it. Help me. Help me believe it.

(HASELTINE *holds out the shoe again.*)

THE DEBBIE: I hate you.

HASELTINE: Yes. (*He takes the shoe from her, hands her shoe back to her, turns his back on her, leans up against the doorway, and puts it on.*)

THE DEBBIE: I hate you and as soon as I believe I hate you, my whole body screams at me, no, he loves you. The things that other people need to have, to prove that someone loves them, you don't need them. You don't need them. Stop asking for them, stop it, stop it, you don't need them.

But you need him. You have to have him. He sees you—he is the only one who has ever seen you, he is the only one who will ever see you. Other people have to guess, but he knows. He is the only one who will ever know.

(HASELTINE *is ready. He starts down the stairs.*)

THE DEBBIE: Please save me. Please save me.

(HASELTINE *is at the bottom of the stairs.*)

THE DEBBIE: God, please save me.

(HASELTINE *is walking away. He is gone.*)

THE DEBBIE: All right. Don't.

(*Lights fade on* THE DEBBIE)

Scene Three

(*The next day, at the lab.*)

(RUTH *enters, carrying some supplies.* JOAN *is standing over* HASELTINE'*s workbench, about to take the blotter off his work.* JOAN *turns quickly when she hears* RUTH *come in, but as soon as she sees that it's* RUTH, *she relaxes.*)

RUTH: What are you doing?

JOAN: What does it look like I'm doing? I work here.

RUTH: That's Haseltine's desk.

JOAN: So?

RUTH: So be careful. You know he doesn't like people looking at his work—what if he comes back in—

JOAN: He's giving a lecture at some conference, some junior college somewhere, left before lunch. Won't be back till late tonight.

RUTH: Yeah?

JOAN: Yeah.

RUTH: (*She goes over to* HASELTINE's *workbench too.*) You're sure?

JOAN: Positive. He took the Kerouac napkin with him. You know what that means.

RUTH: No, I don't, and neither do you.

JOAN: Sure I do. It means he won't be back for a long, long time.

(*Lights up on* HASELTINE, *at a lectern, giving a speech. The area should be isolated from the lab area in such a way that blackouts are not necessary, so that both areas in the scene can work together without fighting for focus.*)

HASELTINE: You must never do something permanent. You must never do something that can't be reversed. If you take a piece of paper, write on it with a pencil, then erase it till the marks are gone, you've still changed that piece of paper forever. The place where you've rubbed away the fibers to remove the lead would always show.

Paper remembers everything that happens to it. Paper remembers it all. So the first thing you do, when you sit down to work, is figure out how you're going to trick that piece of paper. You've got to trick it into letting you work in ways that won't change it, forever. In ways that can be erased so they don't show.

(*They are carefully turning the pages of the manuscript on* HASELTINE's *work area.*)

RUTH: God, it's beautiful. I'd be scared to touch it.

JOAN: You're touching it now.

RUTH: I mean work on it.

JOAN: Come on, you'd love to work on a William Blake—anybody would—

RUTH: Look at how he's done the endpapers he had to replace—he's matched them to the old ones perfectly, except on the new ones there's a shine—see—

JOAN: The same color, the exact same shade, weight—

RUTH: God, he's good. He really is. I mean, any other difference you'd spot immediately—it'd stick out like a sore thumb. But this shine—

JOAN: —is unnatural. How the hell does he do this? You can't get this stuff to shine. (*As* RUTH *turns a few more pages)* He's definitely using one of his strange little concoctions to do this—you know, the little unmarked bottles he hides in the back— (*Rummaging around* HASELTINE*'s workbench)* —probably filled with eyelash of spinster librarian, denatured bookworm bile, heart of remedial reading-level virgin—which he is probably out procuring, right now—

RUTH: Joan—look—there—

JOAN: I don't see anything—

RUTH: There was a big tear, right there—

JOAN: Ruth, there couldn't be—-

RUTH: I saw it yesterday, I saw it when I came over to borrow a couple sheets of mending tissue, it was right here—

JOAN: But—

RUTH: He must have filled it in.

JOAN: Ruth, don't be ridiculous.

RUTH: He did!

JOAN: You're sure it was this page?

(RUTH *nods.*)

JOAN: You're sure the rip was here?

(RUTH *nods again.*)

RUTH: It was an inch and a half, two inches long.

JOAN: Ruth, it would look filled in, it would feel filled in. Nobody can repair a two-inch rip so it doesn't show.

RUTH: He did.

JOAN: He's good. We both know he's good—but nobody's that good.

RUTH: How do you know?

JOAN: Okay then, fine. He's that good. He filled it in. So?

RUTH: So you can't do this sort of thing.

JOAN: Is there something here I'm missing, Ruth, or isn't that what I've been saying all along?

HASELTINE: You must know the strength of the work, and you must not make a repair that is stronger. You must know your materials. If you mend a binding or a page, and use materials that are stronger, the repair itself can stress and damage the work. You must always make a repair just exactly this much— (*He puts his thumb and forefinger together, so there is barely any space between them.*) —weaker than the work itself.

JOAN: It's a probably a new tear, Ruth. A brand new tear. There isn't anything so terribly wrong with repairing something that's not part of the history, you know—

RUTH: How do you know it's new?

JOAN: If it weren't new, Haseltine would have repaired it so we could see it.

RUTH: How do you know?

JOAN: I know Haseltine. Look—maybe he ripped it himself. By accident.

RUTH: Haseltine! Come on.

JOAN: It's possible.

RUTH: Never. Haseltine never did anything wrong to a book in his life.

JOAN: Come on. It could happen. You know no one ever talks about their mistakes.

RUTH: That still doesn't explain how he was able to fill it in like this.

JOAN: Oh, Jesus, Ruth, then ask him when he gets back, just ask him.

RUTH: I can't.

JOAN: Well then you'll have to accept the fact that he just places his hands over the fibers, and wills them to grow.

HASELTINE: You cannot let the beauty, or value, or historical significance of the work get in your way. Unlike a work of art, a book must function. The pages must flex. The folds, the bindings, the cuts must operate. Unlike a work of art, the things you work on were meant to live in the world with us, and it is your job to preserve even the accidents that have happened to it along the way.

RUTH: I think we should talk to someone at the institute about this.

JOAN: I think you should go home and get some rest. Working on the Whitman has obviously affected your mind.

RUTH: I saw it. It was there.

JOAN: Then where is it now?

RUTH: That's not the point.

JOAN: But it is, don't you see that, it is. If he's so good he can fix something so we can't tell how he did it—we can't even tell the repair is there—he's so much better than we are, Ruth. He is. Maybe if we were as good as he is, we'd look at the whole thing differently. You have to look at things differently, with Haseltine.

RUTH: Oh. You mean, if I were good enough, it would be okay for me to break the rules too?

JOAN: Okay, Ruth. Enough. Just stop it.

RUTH: Why? Why should I stop it?

JOAN: Come on, Ruth. You adore Haseltine. It's not like you to be jealous.

RUTH: You think that's what this is? You think I'm jealous of Haseltine?

JOAN: Yes.

RUTH: But you're not.

JOAN: No.

RUTH: Why not?

JOAN: Why should I be jealous of Haseltine? What's the point?

RUTH: Because he's better than you are, and it's human nature to be jealous of people who can do things you want to do and can't.

Unless, of course, you like it this way. Haseltine, King of Conservation. You, Jane.

JOAN: I'm not jealous of you.

RUTH: Of course not! I'm not better than you are. I'm not even as good.

JOAN: Yes you are.

RUTH: Well, at some things—

JOAN: But I still wouldn't be jealous of you unless—
well, I admit it, there is one thing I'd be jealous of, if
you were good enough to do it.

RUTH: What.

JOAN: I'd be jealous if you could find a way to get
through that damn laminate.

RUTH: Oh, no, not the laminate.

JOAN: It's a Yeats love letter, Ruth, it'd be worth being
jealous about. It'd be worth it, to rescue it before the
acid in the cheap cardboard it's laminated to eats it
away. Because the sad thing is, the acid is not just
destroying the letter in patches, a word here, a phrase
there, it's systematically going after the consonants.

RUTH: It is not, and this is not what we're talking
about.

JOAN: It's what I'm talking about.

RUTH: I know what you're doing, Joan. Don't.

JOAN: I can't help it, Ruth, it's true. And it's tragic.
With the consonants gone, all that's left are the vowels,
and what good do a bunch of vowels do you? (*She
has gone over to her workbench, and comes back to* RUTH,
holding a laminated piece of paper.) Here, I'll read you a
sample sentence from the great pen of William Butler
Yeats:
I like calk rings around your head.
That's one possible variation. Here's another:
I lick tall kings around your bed.
Or maybe you prefer this one:
I hike small things around you naked.

(JOAN *looks up, sees* RUTH *trying to repress a smile.*)

JOAN: That was a smile.

RUTH: No it wasn't.

JOAN: Yes it was.

RUTH: It doesn't count, you don't play fair.

JOAN: Of course I don't play fair. Playing fair is your department. You've got tenure, and there's no room for advancement.

RUTH: I hate it when you do this to me.

JOAN: No you don't.

(JOAN *puts her arm around* RUTH, *brings her back to* HASELTINE'*s workbench.*)

JOAN: Come on, help me put everything back exactly the way it was so he won't know we were looking at it.

RUTH: (*Helping her put everything back.*) He'll know anyway.

JOAN: Yes, he always does, but it's worth a try.

(*Lights fade gradually on the lab area.*)

HASELTINE: And the most important thing, and the hardest thing to remember, is this: That the work may not ever be perfect, because perfect is forgery. Everything you do must have your name on it. Every repair you make must stand out clearly as a repair. You know what perfection is, but you do not allow yourself to achieve it.

Give in to perfection, and you have failed.

(*Lights fade slightly on* HASELTINE, *as he walks away from the lectern.*)

(*A* DEBBIE, *this time much younger, comes up to him. She is twenty or so.*)

THE DEBBIE: Excuse me—Mister Haseltine?

HASELTINE: (*Turns to her*) Yes?

THE DEBBIE: I just wanted you to know that I enjoyed your lecture. Very much.

HASELTINE: Thank you.

THE DEBBIE: I don't know that much about book restoration—I mean, conservation—

HASELTINE: They've been drumming that into your heads all day, haven't they? Use restoration, if you like. I've always liked it. It always made me think of that phrase, "restored to life".
  Your name is Debbie, isn't it?

THE DEBBIE: How did you know?

HASELTINE: Sometimes, people look like what they are.

THE DEBBIE: You mean, they look like their name?

HASELTINE: Sometimes. Sometimes, they do.

THE DEBBIE: You think I look like a Debbie?

HASELTINE: Oh, yes. I do. I thought so the minute I saw you.

THE DEBBIE: Can you always tell a person's name like that?

HASELTINE: Me? No. As a matter of fact, Debbies are the only ones.

THE DEBBIE: I hate the name Debbie. I'm thinking of changing it. Which do you like better—

HASELTINE: I like Debbie better.

THE DEBBIE: But you haven't heard the choices yet.

HASELTINE: Still, I like Debbie the best.
  I like you.

THE DEBBIE: (*Some instinct, probably stilled up until now by the fact that* HASELTINE *is old enough to be her father, and the basic trust a young girl has for authority figures, flares to life.*) Well—it's been awfully nice meeting you, I really enjoyed your lecture, and—

HASELTINE: Please don't go—

THE DEBBIE: I really should get going—

HASELTINE: Do you have to?

THE DEBBIE: Well I—yes. I do. Thank you. But—

HASELTINE: You're sure? Because it would just take a half an hour. That's all it would take.

THE DEBBIE: What would?

HASELTINE: For you to help me with some research— but if you have to go—

THE DEBBIE: You're working on something?

HASELTINE: Yes.

THE DEBBIE: Right now? Right here?

HASELTINE: Yes—well, actually, in—
(*He looks around.*)
—in that bar.
(*He points. And waits, looking at her innocently*)

THE DEBBIE: That bar? But— (*It is clear no research could ever be conducted in a bar. Still, she wants to believe.*)
Mister Haseltine? It's a bar.

HASELTINE: (*As if it just suddenly dawns on him too what the problem could be*) Oh, no, I didn't mean—of course not, here, look— (*He opens a small flat case he is carrying, and takes out a cocktail napkin, with something written on it.*) See? It's a passage Jack Kerouac wrote on a bar napkin.

THE DEBBIE: Jack Kerouac! Really?

HASELTINE: Yes. It's not a particularly important Kerouac artifact—but it's a Kerouac all the same. See that ring?

THE DEBBIE: Yes...Oh, I get it—he wrote this in a bar— and that is where his drink left a ring, and—

HASELTINE: Yes. Very good.
   You're pretty, you know that? You're very pretty when you smile.

THE DEBBIE: It would only take a half an hour?

HASELTINE: That's all.

THE DEBBIE: To find out—what are we going to find out?

HASELTINE: What do you think?

THE DEBBIE: To find out—what kind of glass made the ring.

HASELTINE: Very good!

THE DEBBIE: But I don't understand—what difference does it make—either the ring is hurting the napkin, and so you remove it, or it isn't, and you let it stay. Why does it matter what kind of glass made it?

HASELTINE: You really were listening to the lectures, weren't you? Well, let's just say that it wouldn't matter to most people, but that it matters to me.

THE DEBBIE: Your lecture was different too. The others were good, but I liked yours the best.

HASELTINE: Why's that, do you think?

(HASELTINE *and* THE DEBBIE *have stopped, in front of a door. He opens it, stands aside for her to go in.*)

THE DEBBIE: I can only stay a half an hour.

HASELTINE: I know.

(HASELTINE *and* THE DEBBIE *go in. Fade to blackout.*)

Scene Four

(*Night at the lab.* RUTH *is running water into one of the basins, where she will bathe the Whitman pages.* JOAN *is hovering over her, trying to help.*)

RUTH: I wish you'd go home.

JOAN: Ruth, let me help you with that.

RUTH: No. It's my project. Go home.

JOAN: I'm not going home till you do, so you might as well let me help you.

RUTH: I appreciate this, Joan, I do.

JOAN: You haven't let me do anything to appreciate yet. (*She tests the water in the basin, dipping a finger in.*)

RUTH: Well, what you're trying to do.

JOAN: That bath is too cold.

(*Joan tries to take it from* RUTH, *to put hot water in it.* RUTH *pulls it back.*)

RUTH: It is not.

JOAN: It is—

RUTH: Is not!

JOAN: Okay! Okay. But I am still not going home till you do. So there. (*She goes over to the big old easy chair, and flops down in it.*)

RUTH: You're not waiting for me, Joan. Not really. You know it, and I know it. You're waiting for Haseltine to come back.

JOAN: Who me?

RUTH: Yes, you.

JOAN: Well, I appreciate what you're trying to do. But I'm not waiting for him. I'm—taking care of you.

RUTH: What makes you think he's coming back?

JOAN: He's got documents with him, right? Manuscripts, and the napkin. He has to get them back here. I know him. Any normal person would wait and bring them back tomorrow, but not Haseltine.

   And anyway—I repeat. I am not waiting for him. As a matter of fact, I am taking a nap.

RUTH: Joan—

JOAN: I'm napping.

RUTH: This is not fair. You get to tell me what to do but I don't get to tell you.

(JOAN *makes snoring noises.*)

RUTH: Joan, he's out there right now with some bimbo—

JOAN: (*Sitting upright*) Bimbo! BIMBO! Ruth! What would you do if a man called a woman a bimbo in front of you?

RUTH: Spit on him, kick him in the balls, and emasculate him?

JOAN: You would correct him. Gently. Firmly. As I am going to correct you. You must not call the bimbo Haseltine is out with a bimbo. You must call her by her proper noun.

RUTH: Thank you. I stand corrected. He is out there right now with—a Debbie.

JOAN: A—Debbie. (*She throws a dart, perhaps some sort of odd trick shot from the odd angle of the chair.*) I wonder what the Debbies are like. I mean, really. I'd like to talk to one of them someday, get one alone and pump her, you know.

RUTH: About Haseltine?

JOAN: No, of course not. About—being a Debbie. About what it's like to be one. It'd be easy, you know. I see them in the library all the time, hanging around hopefully, with their hair just washed, wearing what they think is the most flattering thing they own. It'd be easy to just walk up to one of them and say, "Hi, Debbie." I mean, that's the way Haseltine does it, right? So it must be easy. I'd find out everything I want to know.

RUTH: From a Debbie?

JOAN: Yeah.

RUTH: But the Debbies don't know anything.

JOAN: Sure they do.

RUTH: If they knew anything, they wouldn't be Debbies.

JOAN: You don't know that. For sure.

RUTH: You know what I think?

JOAN: What.

RUTH: I think you wish you were one.

JOAN: Me? A Debbie?

RUTH: Yeah. I think secretly, deep down inside, you wish you were.

JOAN: You know what I think?

RUTH: What.

JOAN: We are all secret Debbies. (*She throws a dart.*)

RUTH: Not me.

JOAN: Don't be so sure.

RUTH: I'm positive.

JOAN: Okay, so you're the exception that proves the rule. But what's the rule for men, you know, what's a man, deep down inside? I don't have a clue. Because when it comes to men, I always bend the rules.

RUTH: Well, that's the Debbie in you all right.

JOAN: No it isn't—Debbies don't have rules for men. They never make themselves miserable trying to figure out what a man is deep down inside—they don't torture themselves finding out if a man gives a damn about what's right, or taking care of his own, or doing anything in a given day that's bigger than he is. No! They're Debbies! Theirs is not to reason why! Theirs is to dress up in skimpy cocktail dresses, fall head over heels in love with every heel that feels right, and when it's over, have a nice, long, Debbie cry.

RUTH: There's nothing wrong with wanting to see the things you think are right to see in a person, a man—

JOAN: There's plenty wrong with it. Because you know what men look like when I use the rules I think are right? Assholes. Deep down inside, every man I meet looks like an asshole to me.

RUTH: So? Most men, given half a chance, *are* assholes.

JOAN: Yeah, and I'm tired of it. I'm tired of them being assholes. I want them to be men.

RUTH: But Joan—

JOAN: They all look like men to the Debbies, right? So who's got the right way of looking at them—me, or the Debbies?

RUTH: You do, Joan, and you know it.

JOAN: I'm not interested in being reassured that I'm right and the Debbies are wrong, okay? We've been reassuring each other like that for twenty years. Where has it gotten us, Ruth?

RUTH: But you're not wrong. Everybody has their standards, everybody has the things they look for in somebody to love, everybody has—

JOAN: And just because they have them, that means they have to keep them? What happens when it turns out their standards are wrong? When it turns out they got them by—accident? Well, I for one can still walk away from this one. I can just admit I'm using the wrong set of rules about men. I can change.

RUTH: You're being ridiculous. You can't change that kind of thing.

Joan: I'm going to change something inside me, so I can look at them, and see that they are men. (*She sighs.*) And being a Debbie is the only way I know how.

RUTH: You don't even know what you think you're talking about. You don't even know what you think you have to change.

JOAN: Sure I do. Sure I do. After what's real in a person, there is what they want. After what they want is what they have. After what they have, is their hope. Their hope is the very best in them, Ruth.

And my hope is what's wrong with me. There is something wrong with my hope. So that's what I am going to change.

RUTH: Joan—

JOAN: (*Sits back into the chair, closes her eyes, pretends to be sleeping again*) I'm napping.

RUTH: You are not—

JOAN: I am. I'm having deep, sweet, Debbie dreams.

(RUTH *stares at her for a moment, then continues working. She is still bathing the pages of the Whitman manuscript.*)

(*The door opens, and* HASELTINE, *looking a bit the worse for wear, enters carrying several book boxes and a large can of Australian beer.*)

JOAN: (*Without opening her eyes.*) Hiya, Haseltine. You look like shit.

HASELTINE: (*Taking his materials over to his workbench*) You haven't looked at me yet.

RUTH: I think you look like shit too.

HASELTINE: You're not looking at me either. (*He touches the blotter covering the Blake manuscript on his workbench, and adjusts it, carefully.*)

RUTH: I can't look at you. I've got to keep an eye on my historical rust. Make sure it doesn't float away.

HASELTINE: Then why did you say I look like shit?

RUTH: Just being polite.

(HASELTINE *leaves his workbench, goes over to* RUTH'*s.*)

HASELTINE: That bath's too cold.

JOAN: See? I told you so.

RUTH: How can you tell—you can't tell by just looking at it—

HASELTINE: You can tell by the color. And you need a little more of this—

(HASELTINE *hands a bottle of some chemical to her.* RUTH *sprinkles it in, and adds some hot water.*)

HASELTINE: There. You see? It turns a kind of gold, when it's right.

JOAN: It turns piss yellow, when it's right.

HASELTINE: (*Shrugs*) Same thing.

RUTH: (*She takes the page out carefully, blots it with fresh blotters, and puts it next to the pages she had bathed earlier. It is whiter, cleaner, less discolored.*) Damn. Now I have to do them all over again.

HASELTINE: Won't take long, with a little help—

RUTH: No. Thank you, but no.

HASELTINE: Why not?

RUTH: It's my project. You gave it to me. It's mine.

HASELTINE: You can't take a little help from me?

JOAN: Or me either, it seems.

HASELTINE: I see.

JOAN: You do.

HASELTINE: Yes.

JOAN: Then would you mind explaining it to me?

HASELTINE: Well, it's not so strange, is it? It's her project, she's jealous of it. Can't stand for anybody else to touch it. (*He has gone over to his workbench, touches the blotter on top of the Blake.*) Some people are like that, you know. Some people, they don't even like people looking at their work. (*He adjusts the blotter a fraction of an inch, looks up at them, and smiles.*)

RUTH: If I were jealous of anything, it'd be you, Haseltine.

HASELTINE: Me?

RUTH: But I'm not. I'm not saying it's fair, because it isn't fair—

HASELTINE: What isn't fair?

RUTH: It just isn't. But I'm still not jealous.

HASELTINE: If it isn't fair, then you should be jealous. (*He comes over to her, speaks softly.*) I want you to be jealous.

RUTH: You do not. You don't even care. You don't even know what I'm not jealous about.

HASELTINE: So? Jealousy is a primal emotion.

RUTH: Jealousy is an ugly emotion.

HASELTINE: Same thing. It's the perfect emotion, and I want you to have it.

RUTH: You do not.

HASELTINE: But I do. Jealousy is the perfect emotion with which to start our affair.

(HASELTINE *plays at nuzzling her, but doesn't actually touch her.* RUTH *pushes him away with a swing of her hips, as her hands are full. She's more bored than annoyed with his flirting.*)

RUTH: Joan?

JOAN: What?

RUTH: It's not in my contract to fuck Haseltine, is it?

JOAN: No, only the recent hirings have to. You're exempted by the grandfather clause.

RUTH: There. You see?

JOAN: And not only that, but the last time I looked— your name was not Debbie. (*Dart on "Debbie".*)

HASELTINE: (*Wanders off, his hands held up in surrender.*) I give up.

RUTH: You? Never. Even in death. Thirty years from now I'll be standing here, working, wondering where that draft is coming from. I'll look down, and there you'll be. Stone dead on the floor under me. Stone dead, but your soul will be plowing around under my skirt.

HASELTINE: (*He is at her side.*) On its way to heaven at last.

(HASELTINE *reaches a hand, as if to put it up under her skirt— again, he doesn't actually touch her.* RUTH *slaps his hand away with a brush or other implement she is holding.*)

RUTH: There's no heaven under that skirt.

HASELTINE: How do you know?

RUTH: It's been field tested.

HASELTINE: By experts?

JOAN: Lay off, Haseltine. The ink's not even dry on her divorce yet.

HASELTINE: Get back up on the horse that throws you. That's what my daddy always used to say.

RUTH: I didn't know you came from landed gentry, Haseltine. Did you hear that, Joan? Haseltine's a member of the horsey set.

JOAN: No, Ruth. He's just hung like one.

RUTH: Joan!

JOAN: Well, he asked for it.

HASELTINE: Well, if I did it'd be the first thing today I asked for that I got. I'm telling you.

JOAN: Oh, no—I feel a sad story coming on—can it be true? Can it be—say it ain't so—don't tell me, Haseltine—that somewhere in this great metropolis of ours a Debbie has dared to tell you no.

RUTH: That's okay, Haz. You tell your sad story to me. I love your sad stories.

HASELTINE: How could God have made that woman without compassion, that's what I'd like to know. How could he have made her without a heart?

JOAN: I was behind the barn door when he was passing 'em out. Behind the barn door, where I found a pack of women he forgot to give brains to, who were all taking odds on your horse. (*Three darts—on "all", "odds", and "horse"*)

HASELTINE: This is a sad story. Very sad. I'll start at the beginning.

(HASELTINE *begins helping* RUTH. *They work together, putting the Whitman pages in the bath, and taking them out, blotting them.*)

HASELTINE: I met her. Her name was Debbie.

JOAN: They can't all be named Debbie! They just can't!

HASELTINE: I know. But they are. Where was I? I met her. Her name...was Debbie.

(JOAN *and* RUTH *make a rude guffaw.*)

HASELTINE: This is great. You girls are really cheering me up. I get thrown out, on my ass, last night. I have a lousy, luckless day at that conference. I come here for comfort, for solace, to lose myself in my work—

JOAN: In the state you're in, you're lucky you didn't lose your way here.

RUTH: Haseltine, go home. It's late. Go home and go to bed.

HASELTINE: I can't go home and go to bed. That's what I've been trying to tell you. As of last night, I got no bed to go home to.

JOAN: (*Genuinely concerned*) Haseltine—you really got thrown out?

HASELTINE: Sort of.

RUTH: But what about your stuff?

HASELTINE: There isn't much, except my books. I'll go back tomorrow, when she's at work. Get them then.

JOAN: Haseltine, you mind telling me something?

HASELTINE: What?

JOAN: How can you sort of get thrown out?

HASELTINE: I was sort of living with a...friend. So I sort of got thrown out. But that's okay. I got some other friends.

JOAN: Friends?

HASELTINE: Yeah. Any reason why a man shouldn't have a friend who will take him in? A friend in need?

JOAN: A friend who needs her head examined, you mean. So, why are you here? Why are you here, telling your sad story to us instead of to your friend?

HASELTINE: For Christsakes, Joan, it's the middle of the night.

JOAN: So? Seems to me that the middle of the night is when a friend in need comes in so handy.

HASELTINE: Yeah, but handy isn't the problem. The problem is, which one.

JOAN: Which one?

HASELTINE: Yeah. See, there's three of 'em, and it's hard deciding which one to tell my story to. So I thought I'd sleep on it here, wait till tomorrow to make up my mind.

JOAN: Three? You were living with one Debbie, working full time, and you've got three live Debbies on the line?

RUTH: I'll be damned. You are a very busy and resourceful man.

HASELTINE: Well, you got to be resourceful. That's the problem with most of the men who do it. They're not resourceful. They give it a bad name because they do it wrong. And it's important to do it right. Otherwise, what's the point of doing it at all.

And the way to do it right is to take it slow. That way you both know it's happening. That way you both can enjoy it. Men who aren't resourceful can't take it slow, because they never figure out that the only way a man can stand to take it slow is to be taking it, slow, with four or five women at a time.

Sure, there's the main one, the one you're mainly taking it slow with, but the trick is to always be out there, planting those seeds with some new ones. If you don't do that, you'll never get it right, because you'll never learn to love taking it slow.

And that's too bad. Because that's all you really get out of it, you know? Just the waiting, and the wanting. Once you give into it, once it happens, and you've gotten what you've been waiting for, it just goes. You've piled so much on top of it that it just caves in. And it's worse, when it caves in, and you've got no

place else to go. That's why it's important to do it right.
To know how to take it slow.

JOAN: Crop rotation. The cycle of love as seen through
the eyes of Haseltine is nothing but crop rotation.
Tell me. Was it a good year for blondes?

HASELTINE: Hell, I don't care about things like that.

JOAN: Then what do you care about? Assuming you
care. I mean, what are you—a leg man, an ass man, a tit
man?

RUTH: Joan—

JOAN: When did you develop this problem with body
parts, Ruth?

RUTH: When did you?

JOAN: Come on, Haseltine, meet the press. What do
you look for in a woman. I want to know. (*Dart on "I"*)
Ruth wants to know— (*Dart on "Ruth"*)

RUTH: I do not.

JOAN: She's lying, Haseltine. She's dying to know.

RUTH: Leave me out of this, Joan. I'm warning you.

JOAN: You don't want to know?

RUTH: (*Grabbing the darts away from* JOAN) Of course
I want to know. Who wouldn't want to know, really
know, what a man wants, but this is not the way
anyone is going to know. In the first place, no matter
what Haseltine says, it's not going to really tell me, and
in the second, no matter what he says, you'll make it
into a joke, and then we'll go on, and so I won't know,
so what's the point? What's the point in wanting to
know something you can't know! (*Three darts, on
"point", "know", and "know"*)

JOAN: I don't make everything into a joke, Ruth—

RUTH: You do so. You don't know anything that isn't funny. No matter what we talk about it always ends up as a joke.

JOAN: That's not true, Ruth—I know I used to be like that, but not anymore—

RUTH: No, not when we're talking about your problems, about what you need, but when we talk about mine, when we talk about what I need— (*She stops, goes back to work, putting things away in a quiet, angry way.*)

JOAN: Haseltine?

HASELTINE: What?

JOAN: Can you tell Ruth what you look for in a woman?

HASELTINE: Maybe.

JOAN: No, I mean really tell her. So she'll know.

HASELTINE: I look at her heart. That's the first thing I see when I look at a woman. Her heart. Sure, there's leg men and ass men and tit men. But that's what they are. That's what they get. They only get a piece of it. You want it all. So first thing you got to look at is her heart. Which is, I admit, intimated...occasionally, when you get that first look at the legs or tits or ass. But is only seen inside her. You see her heart. You see how big it is. And you decide.

JOAN: Am I allowed to say something funny if it is also sad?

RUTH: No.

JOAN: Am I allowed to say something sad, if it's not funny?

RUTH: Say whatever the hell you like, Joan.

JOAN: I think that is the saddest thing I've ever heard. I think you want to see how big their hearts are so you can break them.

HASELTINE: (*Shrugs*) That's okay. You asked me. I told you. That's okay.

RUTH: I'm going. Goodnight.

JOAN: I'm going with you. It's too late for you to walk home alone.

RUTH: Suit yourself.

JOAN: Haseltine, come on. I want you to come home with me. Stay at my place. I don't want you staying here.

HASELTINE: Thanks, but I'll sleep on that chair over there. I've done it before. Chances are I'll end up doing it again.

JOAN: You can't stay here. Ruth, tell him he can't.

RUTH: Why not?

JOAN: It doesn't look right.

RUTH: It doesn't look right? To who? Emily Post?

JOAN: And he'll never get any sleep on that chair.

RUTH: He says he sleeps on it all the time.

JOAN: I don't care. It's not right. We can't leave him to sleep on that chair.

RUTH: All right. Okay. Haseltine—I've got more room than Joan does. Come home with me.

JOAN: He can't go home with you.

RUTH: Why not?

JOAN: Because he just can't.

RUTH: He can go home with you, but he can't go home with me?

HASELTINE: I don't want to go home with either one of you.

RUTH: All you've got is that horrid fold-out couch, Joan, I've got a guest room and—
  Oh. Funny the things you forget.
  Looks like you're going home with Joan, Haseltine. My husband got the guest room, since it was attached to the house. I'm staying with my mother—who has a very big heart—but a very traditional one.

HASELTINE: I'd rather just stay here.

RUTH: You don't stand a chance, Haseltine. She always gets her way when it comes to things like this.

HASELTINE: I'd still rather not.

JOAN: Why not? It's safe. I've got no heart. You said so yourself. So if I've got no heart, there's nothing to see. Nothing to break.

HASELTINE: No heart?

JOAN: That's right.

HASELTINE: No heart.
  Let's go.

(*Lights fade on the lab area, as the three of them leave together.*)

Scene Five

(JOAN *and* HASELTINE *and* RUTH *are walking along the street. There is a late-night sound and feel to it.*)

RUTH: Well—thanks for walking me.

(*They stop at* RUTH's *mother's house. We see only the barest suggestion of the white fence around the house, the walkway up to the front door.*)

HASELTINE: Goodnight.

JOAN: 'Night. Tell your mom hi for me.

RUTH: I will. (*She goes off stage, into the house.*)

JOAN: And don't forget to take a bath.

RUTH (*Offstage:*) Joan—

JOAN: I mean it, Ruth, or your shoulder will freeze up—

RUTH: (*Comes back out, very definite about things*) I'll take one in the morning, it's too late—

JOAN: I am going to stand here *yelling* until I hear you start the water for your bath, Ruth. I am.

RUTH: Then you are going to stand there a very long, long time.
    'Night again, Haseltine.

HASELTINE: 'Night.

(RUTH *leaves again.*)

JOAN: (*Pause. Yelling:*) I don't hear anything, Ruth.

HASELTINE: Joan?

JOAN: What.

HASELTINE: It's kinda late.

JOAN: So? Her shoulder will freeze up if she doesn't take a bath.

HASELTINE: So, you're gonna wake up the whole neighborhood.

JOAN: Oh, I'm not gonna wake up the whole neighborhood.

HASELTINE: You're not?

JOAN: No. Bruno is. (Yelling) *Ruthieeeeeeeee...I don't hear the water!*

HASELTINE: Bruno?

JOAN: Bruno. We should have killed him when we had the chance. (Yelling) *Ruth we should have killed him when we had the chance.* See, the dog starts barking, wakes up the whole neighborhood everytime Ruth—*Ruth! Ruthie? I don't hear it, Ruth! (She listens intently.)* Haseltine—you hear water running?

HASELTINE: Nope.

JOAN: Neither do I. (*A dog begins frantic barking.)* But Bruno does. *(Yelling, to Ruth.)* Goodnight, Ruth—*enjoy your bath.*

(*The dog barks louder.* JOAN *pulls* HASELTINE *along. They start walking again, strolling, enjoying the evening.)*

HASELTINE: Why'd you do that?

JOAN: (*Shrugs)* She's my best friend.

HASELTINE: So?

JOAN: So...I'm taking care of her.

HASELTINE: Oh. So that's what you call it.

(HASELTINE *and* JOAN *walk a step or two.)*

HASELTINE: You would drive me crazy.

JOAN: Would I?

HASELTINE: Hell, yes. I think that's what would drive me nuts about you, ultimately. The way you'd take care of me.

JOAN: You'd be surprised.

HASELTINE: Not that there's anything wrong with someone taking care of someone. If that's what she wants.

JOAN: Do the Debbies take care of you?

HASELTINE: Sometimes. Sometimes, you have to let them take care of you.

JOAN: Until it drives you crazy, of course.

HASELTINE: Of course.

JOAN: (*They stop in front of the door to* JOAN's *apartment.*) What would it be like, Haseltine?

HASELTINE: You taking care of me?

JOAN: No, if I were a Debbie.

HASELTINE: You're not a Debbie.

JOAN: But if I were a Debbie—

HASELTINE: You're not—

JOAN: But if I were a Debbie, and we were going home, like this.
   What would it be like?

HASELTINE: This your place?

JOAN: Yeah.

HASELTINE: Open the door.

JOAN: Haz, I asked you a question.

HASELTINE: Open the door.

JOAN: Haseltine—

HASELTINE: Open the door. I'll answer it. You'll see.

(JOAN *opens the door.*)

(*Blackout*)

END OF ACT ONE

ACT TWO

Scene One

(JOAN *and* HASELTINE, *as at the end of* ACT ONE.)

(HASELTINE *looks the staircase up and down. It is an old, wooden staircase, with a beautiful railing, not restored. He nods his head and smiles, as if to say "good, good".)*

(JOAN *closes the door behind them.* HASELTINE *takes her by both shoulders, and spins her, slowly, in a kind of waltz, to the staircase and up one or two of the stairs.)*

(HASELTINE *kisses* JOAN. *She lets him. She is not so much kissing him, as tasting what kissing him would be like.)*

(HASELTINE *stops, leans* JOAN *up against the railing, and holds her, stroking her arms from the elbow to the shoulder, up and down.)*

HASELTINE: You know what the French say about this?

JOAN: No.

HASELTINE: The French say, "It is never as good as it is when you are first climbing the stairs."

JOAN: Well, the French should know.

HASELTINE: They say this, of course, because— *(He lunges at her; she plays with him; they progress up another stair.)* —the French, as you know, have no ranch houses. No split levels. There is no poetry in the staircase of a split-level home. *(They are at it again.* JOAN *pulls away from him; they are up another stair.)*

Jazz. Musical comedy. And split levels. The three
indigenous American art forms.

(This time HASELTINE *is the one who plays with* JOAN. *They
are up another stair, cat and mouse.)*

HASELTINE: You didn't know the split-level home
was an American invention? No, I'll bet you didn't.
But it is. Next to jazz, it is our single most important
contribution. It was invented after jazz, which is why
the staircases in them are so damned unromantic.
    We shot our wad on jazz. *(Another step, stalking her.
They aren't touching, at the moment.)*

HASELTINE: I don't know a thing about jazz, by the
way. *(Another step, still stalking)* It is one of those
regrettable...gaps...in my sophistication.

*(They are at the top of the landing. They kiss, they grope,
they gobble each other up.)*

*(*JOAN *pushes him away. She catches her breath.* HASELTINE
*starts toward her; she shakes her head, "No". He backs up
against the wall, stunned.)*

HASELTINE: What's wrong?

JOAN: Nothing's wrong.

HASELTINE: Look—maybe I misunderstood you, but—

JOAN: What could be wrong? I am in complete
agreement with the French. Except when it comes to
their politics, of course. Their anti-Semitism. Their
dirty dealings with the Arabs. That sort of thing.
    Don't look at me like that, Haseltine. Just because we
spend our days preserving the work of great men of
the past doesn't mean we can't be semi-aware of the
work of great assholes in the present.

HASELTINE: You have some problem with the French?

JOAN: No, nothing out of the ordinary, I expect.

HASELTINE: Look, this was your idea—you want to stop, okay, but—

JOAN: Haseltine—that's a French name, isn't it? I never thought of you as being French. But it makes a lot of sense. You are, after all, the one who said it.

HASELTINE: What.

JOAN: It is never as good as it is when you are first climbing the stairs.

HASELTINE: So?

JOAN: So...it was good. Really good. It was fabulous. Thank you.

HASELTINE: You're welcome. So?

JOAN: So—I once spent a week with a man named Charles at one of those useless bookbinder conventions—everybody sharing the recipe for the perfect nonbinding glue, that sort of thing. It was spring, which in France means one thing, but in Nebraska, it means another. It means tornadoes. So, when the convention was over, our plane took off right into the middle of one. Half of all the really big guns in book conservation were on that plane, and I was imagining the headlines if it went down. LIBRARIANS PAY THE BIG FINE. And, PLANE OVERDUE. That sort of thing.

I was having an excellent time.

I knew that to die with that week I had spent with Charles inside me—to die, not full of fear, or longing, or regret, but full of that—that would be heaven.

I don't believe in heaven, do you?

(HASELTINE *starts to reply;* JOAN *keeps rolling.*)

Joan: The French do, I suppose. But the airplane is an American invention. Which explains a lot of things.

(HASELTINE *again tries to say something;* JOAN *cuts him off.*)

JOAN: Anyway, I didn't die—so much for my one shot at heaven—and, since staircases don't crash—we have to take responsibility ourselves. You said it is never as good as it is when you are first climbing the stairs. I agree.

But the stairs didn't crash. We missed our chance.

That was as good as it was ever going to get. Why go on?

Can I get you something to drink? Juice? Water out of a bottle? Or something more...binding? Something that will bind itself to your red blood cells, make its way to your brain, and erase a few choice entries from those soft gray pages?

HASELTINE: I think I liked it better when I thought this was just some problem you were having with the French.

JOAN: Really? Well, thank you. If I believed you I'd take that as a compliment.

HASELTINE: What's that supposed to mean?

JOAN: Oh, not much. Except I make it a rule. Never to believe a word a man says when he has a raging hard-on.

HASELTINE: You...have got to be kidding.

JOAN: No. Why would I be? I admit that it isn't really raging, not at this point. But it's still quite respectable. Look for yourself.

HASELTINE: I don't have to look! We both know it's there and we both know where it came from. I didn't exactly get it at Macy's, you know!

JOAN: Yes, but if you had you could return it. After all, it hasn't been used.

HASELTINE: Am I crazy? Am I nuts? Wasn't that you, with me, just a few minutes ago, on the stairs?

JOAN: Oh, so you think it's my fault? My responsibility?

HASELTINE: Yeah. I do. It was your idea.

JOAN: Please—spare me. You think women don't have hard-ons—figuratively speaking—too? It'll go away. The law of gravity, and all. What goes up must then come down. And if you're in too much of a hurry to wait for the great, natural order of things to take care of it for you, you could always hit it a couple times.

HASELTINE: Hit it?

JOAN: It makes it kind of numb—that's my understanding, anyway. Hit it. I imagine it will hurt a little bit. Like wearing high heels. You'll be thrilled when it goes away.

HASELTINE: *(Pause. Then—he finds a handle, a way back to the familiar. As always, when he discovers the way to make what is happening into a seduction, he's on again.)* You hit it.

JOAN: Me?

HASELTINE: Yeah. It's your idea. You hit it.

(JOAN seems to be playing along with HASELTINE. He thinks he knows the game. He comes closer, as she speaks. They dance around the room a bit.)

JOAN: I couldn't.

HASELTINE: Sure you could.

JOAN: But I've never done anything like that before.

HASELTINE: Sorry. I'd like to believe you. But I make it a rule. Never to believe a word anybody says when they've got a figurative hard-on.

JOAN: Good point. Still, the sad truth is, I'm just not that kind of girl.

HASELTINE: If you've never tried, then how do you know?

JOAN: Because I've...read about girls like that.

HASELTINE: In books?

JOAN: Yes. Books.

HASELTINE: How sad. How very, very sad. In the good old days of censorship, girls were never allowed to read books about girls like that, and so consequently were more open to suggestion. I mean—experience.

JOAN: I'm not saying I wouldn't like to have the enriching experience of first-hand knowledge...the benefits of a hands-on atmosphere—

HASELTINE: You get the picture.

JOAN: There weren't usually pictures in the books I read, Haseltine. You're thinking about pornography.
    Still, on the other hand, the works of the Marquis de Sade are classics, as well as being French, and you know how I feel about the French—

HASELTINE: *Hit it or don't hit it but so help me God if you start in on the French again I'm going to lose my mind!!!!!*

JOAN: All right. I'll hit it. Close your eyes and turn around.

HASELTINE: Now wait a minute—

JOAN: Just so I can get...ready.

HASELTINE: Ready?

JOAN: Yes. I want this one to be by the book.

(HASELTINE *turns around, closes his eyes.* JOAN *turns, grabs a big atlas from one of the overflowing bookcases, and takes a nice practice swipe.)*

JOAN: I'm ready. You can open your eyes and turn around.

HASELTINE: *(He does.) Shit—*

(HASELTINE *runs away from* JOAN, *never turning his back on her, shielding his crotch, trying to grab the book away. They romp around the room, she just barely able to keep a straight face, he not quite sure this is happening to him. She takes many wide, wild swipes.)*

JOAN: Stand still, Haseltine.

HASELTINE: Put that thing down.

JOAN: But I like it, Haz, I like it. Just like you said I would.

HASELTINE: This isn't funny—this is insane—

JOAN: You try to do a man a favor—

HASELTINE: Yeah, well, don't do me no more favors, okay—

JOAN: *(Singing, swaying to the music, the atlas poised in readiness above her head.)* "She's got the whole wo-rld (the known world, that is) in her hands." *(She continues singing/humming, over/under* HASELTINE *and herself.)*

HASELTINE: *You're crazy!*

JOAN: You *begged* me!

HASELTINE: You drove me to it—you and the goddamn French—

JOAN: The French—oh, Lord, I almost forgot—

(JOAN *opens the atlas, and rips out a few pages.* HASELTINE *stares at her for a moment, astonished. He moves toward her.)*

JOAN: I've excised the offending continent—except for Morocco, you will not be touched by anything even remotely—

(HASELTINE *grabs the atlas away from* JOAN. *She collapses, laughing.*)

JOAN:—French. Oh, God *Haseltine*!! The look on your face.

(HASELTINE *holds up the atlas, as if about to strike* JOAN *with it.*)

JOAN: Oh, God, I'm gonna be sick. Oh, God.

HASELTINE: (*Sits down, opens the atlas, and looks through it gently*) I hope you are sick. I hope you're laugh-your-guts-out sick.

JOAN: (*Rolling around on the floor, laughing*) Oh, do you really, Haseltine, do you? I hope not, Haseltine. Because you know what? (*She peeks under the atlas he's holding in his lap.*) It worked! It's all gone. (*She lies down on her back, on the floor.*) Oh, Haseltine. Is it always this much fun being a Debbie?

HASELTINE: That was your idea of fun?

JOAN: Fun? It was glorious! I got Tom Haseltine to dance around the room holding his nuts while I sang spiritual hymns.

HASELTINE: I looked pretty...ridiculous....

JOAN: You? Oh, no— (*She bursts into a new attack of laughter.*)

HASELTINE: (*He starts laughing too.*) Oh, Jesus. I must have looked like—oh, God—

JOAN: "I've got the whole world...." (*She's laughing too hard to continue.*)

HASELTINE: Oh, God, you can't tell anyone at work—

JOAN: *Oh my lord—think of what they'd pay!*

HASELTINE: Promise me you won't tell—

JOAN: I promise, I promise—except Ruth, I have to tell Ruth, she's my best friend—

HASELTINE: You promise me!

JOAN: Okay. Okay. Oh. *(She calms down, but is still laughing softly.)* I promise. No matter what. Even after you turn out to be the biggest shit that ever lived.

(JOAN is still smiling and laughing, but HASELTINE has stopped.)

JOAN: Even after you break me in two and throw out the pieces.

(They have both stopped laughing.)

JOAN: I won't tell.

HASELTINE: *(Moving away from her.)* Why'd you have to spoil it?

JOAN: Spoil what?

HASELTINE: We were having a good laugh. Such a good laugh. I haven't had a good laugh like that—

JOAN: Haseltine, I work with you. I hear all the stories. I know what you are. What's wrong with saying, flat out: I know what you are.

HASELTINE: You know what you are? A goddamn tease.

JOAN: *(Gets up, follows him.)* No. Emphatically not. But you are.

HASELTINE: I am not!

JOAN: I don't mean a tease like that, Haseltine. I mean—see, Haseltine, you know all these things. Things I want to know. You're a tease when it comes to that. To things I want to know.

HASELTINE: You mean—at work.

JOAN: Well, sure, a little bit. But they're your techniques—it's your...business who you want to show. What I'm talking about is...stuff. About the world. You know all this shit. I don't know how you know it, or what you know, exactly, but I want to know it. I want you to show me.

HASELTINE: Last thing I tried to show you, you went after with an atlas.

JOAN: Seriously, Haseltine. I think you know stuff I need to know.

HASELTINE: And you want me to...show you.

JOAN: Yeah.

HASELTINE: You can do it just like that? You can come up to a man, and say, "Show me what you know," and he'll show you?

JOAN: Why not? Why wouldn't he?

HASELTINE: It doesn't work like that.

JOAN: Why not?

HASELTINE: You ever done this before? Ever asked a man home, gotten him hot on the stairs, then said, "Please put that thing away, and show me what you know?"

JOAN: No, but—

HASELTINE: That proves it.

JOAN: All it proves is I never met a man who knew anything before.
    How about you?

HASELTINE: Me? I never ask for knowledge. I stick with what I know.

JOAN: Hasn't anyone ever asked you? Haven't any of the dozens and dozens of Debbies ever asked you this before?

HASELTINE: Nope. Not a one.

JOAN: That is where you are wrong. That is where you are painfully, tragically, incorrect. (Pause) But, on the other hand, I'm not really a Debbie, am I?

So maybe I'm the one who is painfully, tragically incorrect.

(JOAN *turns, and begins removing the cushions from the sofa, stacking them on the floor so that she can unfold the hide-a-bed.* HASELTINE *watches her carefully.*)

HASELTINE: What if I were the one asking you to put that figurative thing away, and show me what you know.

JOAN: You'd be out of luck.

HASELTINE: Why?

JOAN: Because the things I know I don't believe in anymore.

(*Joan pulls out the sofa bed. It is perfectly made up, with pillows, and a small stack of towels, and a little bar of guest soap, and a toothbrush, etc. She looks at it all.*)

JOAN: The attraction of order out of chaos is strong in a librarian. Very strong.

(JOAN *gets busy turning down the bed, plumping up the pillows.* HASELTINE *watches her carefully.*)

JOAN: Sometimes I look at the things around me, the way I lead my life, the order, the evidence, and I think—God, who lives this life. What is she scared of. What difference can it make. (*She is through.*) I don't have to talk like this, you know. I can stop it, if you like. (*No response from* HASELTINE. *She turns and leaves.*) Goodnight.

HASELTINE: (*Touches the pillows*) Goodnight.

(*Fade to blackout*)

Scene Two

(Morning. HASELTINE *is sitting on the edge of the hide-a-bed as* JOAN *enters.* HASELTINE *is wearing his pants, but not his shirt.* JOAN *is on her way into the kitchen to make coffee.)*

JOAN: I dreamed about you last night.

HASELTINE: You did.

JOAN: Well, sort of about you. I dreamed my wings were being eaten by a Debbie.

HASELTINE: You had wings?

JOAN: Yes. The Debbie was eating them.

HASELTINE: Oh.

JOAN: *(Coming back from the kitchen.)* Do you think that's a normal sort of dream for me to have, or not? I mean—are the Debbies unusually big eaters? Or is it just that you don't feed them enough?

*(*JOAN *sits on the bed next to* HASELTINE.*)*

HASELTINE: You have wings a lot in your dreams?

JOAN: Well, not every night. Occasionally.

HASELTINE: I had a dream once where I ate sandwiches made out of my own flesh.

JOAN: Flesh sandwiches?

HASELTINE: Yeah. Someone kept handing them to me.

JOAN: Flesh sandwiches...well. How'd they taste?

*(*HASELTINE *kisses the back of* JOAN'*s neck.)*

HASELTINE: Terrible.

JOAN: *(Didn't hear him)* What?

HASELTINE: I said they tasted about the same as your wings did. *(Softer, as he kisses her again.)* Terrible. *(He *kisses her again. He takes her hand, and tries to put it on his crotch.)* There's someone I'd like you to meet.

JOAN: *(She did hear him.)* Excuse me?

HASELTINE: There's someone—

JOAN: I heard you. You are a grown man, Haseltine. You are too old to be anthropomorphizing your dick. *(She grabs her hand back.)*

HASELTINE: And what are you too old for?

JOAN: To believe that it would be anything but hell to get involved with a man like you.

HASELTINE: But you want to? Just a little bit?

JOAN: A little bit.

HASELTINE: Why's that?

JOAN: *(She pulls away from him.)* I'm not going to sleep with you, Haseltine.

HASELTINE: Yes you are.

JOAN: I'm not. Not now. Not yet.

HASELTINE: You're too old for this one, Joan.

JOAN: For what?

HASELTINE: Trust me. I know this one. This one is called, "If I don't give in right away, maybe I'll get him for good."

JOAN: Get you for good? *What the hell would I do with you!!*

HASELTINE: I don't believe you.

JOAN: Believe me.

HASELTINE: I wish I could. But that's the trouble with these figurative hard-ons. You can never be sure they've gone away. They sometimes can last for months. Even years. I've seen one that's lasted almost three years.

JOAN: What makes you so sure you can see it?

HASELTINE: I'm sure.

JOAN: Good. Good for you.

HASELTINE: You know, in a way it's very comforting, to see that you have this hope. Yes, it's comforting. To see that a woman, at your age—

JOAN: Thank you.

HASELTINE: I mean—with your—maturity—wisdom— experience—that a woman who has had and seen and done all you have can still have faith in the eternal "not yet", in the implied "later", in that better world a woman imagines she can build around a man out of the power the word "no"has when she knows both of you know it means yes.
  It's a gift, to have that much faith in a word. A gift. But I don't have it.
  There's only one difference between now and later. And that's that I'm here now.

(HASELTINE *kisses Joan.*)

HASELTINE: Now you say you want to know something? Well, here's the guy who knows.

(HASELTINE *places* JOAN*'s hand on his crotch. She doesn't exactly resist.*)

HASELTINE: Oh, he's seen the sights all right. Been inside a couple hundred wonders of the world. Been absolutely everywhere there is for a guy like him to go. Gets into places so goddamn well fortified, the great Houdini could learn a thing or two, if he were still alive. But he wouldn't tell Houdini how he does it. They're his techniques. It's his business who he shows.
  But I have the feeling that he might show you. If you ask him nicely.

(JOAN *takes her hand off* HASELTINE *and steps back.*)

HASELTINE: Don't go now —don't—you got this great big burning thirst for knowledge. Don't tell me it's all burned out.

JOAN: *(Shaking her head in amazement)* Does this sort of thing really work with the Debbies?

HASELTINE: What do the Debbies have to do with this, come on, ask him—

JOAN: You are incredible. Just incredible. Anybody ever tell you that?

HASELTINE: Yeah. Usually not at this point in the narrative, but—

JOAN: Oh, but now or later, before or after, as long as they say you're incredible, it's the same thing to you?

HASELTINE: No. Now or later, not the same. *(He turns away from her, grabs his shirt, puts it on.)* I thought you understood that.

I thought—maybe—you understood me.

(JOAN takes a step toward HASELTINE, then stops.)

JOAN: Oh, no you don't. You're not going to do this to me. *(She starts to pace a bit.)*

HASELTINE: Do what? You're the one doing something. Or not doing something. You're the one who's done this to me twice. *(He starts buttoning his shirt, grabs his tie.)*

JOAN: *(Leaning against something, casually)* You're not going anywhere, Haseltine.

HASELTINE: I'm not? Correct me if I'm wrong—but doesn't it look like I'm leaving?

JOAN: Oh, I admit, to the novice, to the neophyte, it might appear that you're leaving. But I know you. I know how you work. It might look, to the run-of-the-mill Debbie, like you're on your way out that door— but those who know you know—you don't ever stop

what you've started till you've finished it.
  And I know you.

HASELTINE: Do you?

JOAN: Yeah, I do. And it would eat you up, Haseltine.
It would eat on you forever to know that what I want
to say is yes. But you weren't good enough to get me to
say it.

(HASELTINE *is almost out the door.*)

JOAN: So all you got was no.

HASELTINE: *(He stops, cold, in the doorway.)* Yeah. You
know me. *(Shaking his head, he comes back.)* Nobody
else—none of them know me. But you do.

JOAN: Oh, please don't, Haseltine. Please don't say that.

HASELTINE: What do you mean, don't say it, you just
said it—

JOAN: Yes, but I didn't mean it—

HASELTINE: Then why did you say it—

JOAN: Damn it. Damn it. I know what you want. I
know what you're trying to do to me. I know you can't
change.

HASELTINE: Who said anything about changing?

JOAN: *(Screaming)I know better than this, damnit, I
know!!!!*
  I'm not going to let you do this to me.

HASELTINE: Jesus, I'm not trying to do anything to
you—I don't even know what you think I'm trying to
do.

JOAN: From the first minute you walked in that door at
work I've been in love you. Three years. Three stupid,
stupid years.
  I know better than this. After three years of Debbie
stories, I must be out of my mind.

HASELTINE: That's good, right? That means yes, right?

JOAN: No. A woman who loves a man owes it to him
to—

HASELTINE: Well, that sounds like yes—

JOAN: A woman who loves a man owes it to him to
know he can't change.

HASELTINE: Look, I haven't said a word about
changing—

JOAN: Because I know you can't.

HASELTINE: I don't want to change.

JOAN: Good. Because people don't change.

HASELTINE: I never said they did.

JOAN: Even if they want to. Even if it's the most
important thing in the world to them. They can't
change.
   What happens to the Debbies when you're through
with them?

HASELTINE: I don't know.

JOAN: You don't care?

HASELTINE: I didn't say that.

JOAN: You do care?

HASELTINE: Why would I do it if I didn't care?

JOAN: I don't know.

HASELTINE: You think there's no point to it? I just do it
and do it, for no reason at all?

JOAN: No reason that has anything to do with them.

HASELTINE: That's where you're wrong. The reason to
it, the point to it all—is to give them something.

JOAN: Yeah, right, I know what you give them.

HASELTINE: That's not what I mean—

JOAN: The Lord giveth, and the Lord taketh away.

HASELTINE: The point is to give them something they can keep, after I'm gone. The point is to give them something that stays.

JOAN: But you don't.

HASELTINE: No.

JOAN: Then it isn't real.

HASELTINE: Who says it's not.

JOAN: If it's real you stay.

HASELTINE: That's what you say. That's what they say. But staying is not the point. Anyone can stay. It's what you do to them—give them—that's what's important. That's what you want to say. Can you understand that?

JOAN: No.

HASELTINE: Sure you can.

JOAN: I don't want to.

HASELTINE: This is what you said you wanted to know, Joan.

JOAN: I said I don't want to!

HASELTINE: Don't be a tease, Joan. This is the thing you said you wanted to know.

They walk by me. And I can see there's something about them that doesn't make sense, like they've put the wrong pieces together. They walk by me, and everything they do seems to hurt some other part of them. Like they have lost something. Or forgotten it. But I see it.

(HASELTINE *has gone to one of the landings as a* DEBBIE, *perhaps in her middle thirties, walks out, carrying a stack of library books. She looks around for a place to sit down. They are in the garden at the library.*)

HASELTINE: I see it, there, inside her, where she's hiding it, protecting it. Saving it, for something. I see it, and I don't do anything to her, really. I just let something in her out.

(HASELTINE *walks up to* THE DEBBIE. *She is sitting cross-legged, reading, playing absently with her hair.*)

HASELTINE: Excuse me?

THE DEBBIE: Yes?

HASELTINE: You shouldn't do that.

THE DEBBIE: Shouldn't do what—sit here on the grass?

HASELTINE: It's all right, to sit on the grass.

THE DEBBIE: Then what is the problem?

HASELTINE: That book.

THE DEBBIE: What about it?

HASELTINE: You shouldn't be reading it out here.

THE DEBBIE: Guess what, Mister? This is a library.

HASELTINE: I know, but—

THE DEBBIE: Look—would you mind leaving me alone?

HASELTINE: No. I can't.

THE DEBBIE: (*Gathers up her things, getting ready to leave*) Excuse me—

HASELTINE: No, wait—I'm a librarian—

THE DEBBIE: (*Continuing to get ready*) You don't look like a librarian.

HASELTINE: You ever look at a librarian? Really look at one?

THE DEBBIE: No one really looks at librarians, you know.

HASELTINE: So. As it turns out, you can't tell me one thing about what a librarian looks like.

THE DEBBIE: *(Can't help smiling)* No. I suppose not.

HASELTINE: *(To* JOAN*)* You see? See how it's starting already? See how she starts to shine? *(To* THE DEBBIE*)* Trust me. I look like a librarian.

THE DEBBIE: All right.

HASELTINE: And you look like...a Debbie.

THE DEBBIE: How did you know?

HASELTINE: I know because you do.

THE DEBBIE: Wait a minute—you saw me checking these books out—you looked in the computer, you found my name, followed me out here, ruined my day—

HASELTINE: I don't even know how to use the computer.

THE DEBBIE: A librarian who doesn't know how to use the computer the entire library system is on? Come on!

HASELTINE: *(To* JOAN*)* See how she's starting to close up? She doesn't really want to, but she's thinking she should. *(To* THE DEBBIE*)* Librarians are like doctors— we're all specialists. Experts, in one particular field. Some of us—check books out. Some of us—check books in. Some of us do nothing but patrol the stacks going "Shhhhhh. It's a library."

 I'm a conservator—I don't do any of those things.

*(*HASELTINE *takes* THE DEBBIE*'s book away from her, closing it.)*

THE DEBBIE: Hey—you lost my place—

HASELTINE: No—

THE DEBBIE: You did too—

HASELTINE: I didn't. Look— *(He balances the book in one hand, holding the spine in the palm of his hand. The book falls open by itself.)* See?

THE DEBBIE: How'd you do that?

HASELTINE: Would you believe I have a strange and mysterious power over books?

THE DEBBIE: No.

HASELTINE: You wouldn't?

THE DEBBIE: Absolutely not.

HASELTINE: Well, you might be right. But as it turns out, I was watching when you sat down and opened this book. And I noticed that you had broken the spine.

THE DEBBIE: I did not hurt that book—

HASELTINE: It's all right—

THE DEBBIE: I love books. Ever since I was little, I've always been careful with them. Always.

HASELTINE: It's all right. I'll show you the right way to open them.

(HASELTINE *puts the book in* THE DEBBIE'*s left hand, and bends over her, putting his right hand over hers, to guide it.*)

HASELTINE: Take it like this—hold it loosely, yes, that's it. And with your right hand, go in, forty pages or so, with the side of your hand, starting at the top, close up next to the binding, press firmly, draw your hand down. All right. Good. Now go forty pages or so more, and keep going till you're done.

(HASELTINE *lets go of* THE DEBBIE'*s hands, lets her continue working alone.*)

HASELTINE: *(To* JOAN:*)* She knows better. You know she does. Sometimes that's the part you like best about her. The part that's telling her that if she knows what's good for her, she'll run. It's the part you like the best because it's the part she trusts. The part of herself she trusts the most.

The part you know, sooner or later, she'll trust to

you.

   She will trust you with the most beautiful things about herself she knows.

THE DEBBIE: It's really important to open a book like this?

HASELTINE: Very.

THE DEBBIE: Then how come no one ever told me before?

HASELTINE: I told you.

THE DEBBIE: Yes. Thank you. Thank you for showing me.

HASELTINE: Would you like me to show you a place inside you could read? Comfortable, nice, high ceilings, tucked away. Most people don't know about it.

THE DEBBIE: Thank you, no. That's okay. Maybe some other time. I'll just stay out here.

HASELTINE: *(To* JOAN*)* See—there she goes again, shutting down. She doesn't want me to see it for too long. I might steal it.

THE DEBBIE: I like it out here.

HASELTINE: She knows. She's been warned. But she can't quite keep herself from hoping.

THE DEBBIE: It's one of the things I like best—reading outside. All this light.

HASELTINE: All this light.

(HASELTINE *takes the book from* THE DEBBIE *again.)*

HASELTINE: Did you know that a page in this book is like your skin?

(HASELTINE *touches* THE DEBBIE'S *cheek, just for an instant.)*

HASELTINE: Not as soft, maybe, but it ages just as fast, in the sunlight. A piece of paper ages a month in an hour in the sun.

THE DEBBIE: It does?

HASELTINE: Most people don't know it, but it does Come on. I'll show you that room.

(THE DEBBIE *picks up her books and they go down the steps together.* THE DEBBIE *goes offstage, and* HASELTINE *returns to* JOAN.)

HASELTINE: And I take her to that room. And I leave her. But she comes back. And each time she does, she changes, faster and faster. She runs into me, by accident, in the parking lot. In the front room. By the stairs. She looks up at me—and she's not afraid. She's beautiful. So goddamn beautiful. And then—I can't help it. I have to—have that, don't I? I have to—she's so beautiful, I have to take some of that back. It's mine, I gave it to her, I have to...
    If I could just stop—there—before I have to—touch it, take it back—if I could just freeze it, preserve it, just there, with her looking up from the book she's pretending to read, or that moment she sees me when she's coming down the stairs—if I could stop there, with that secret thing inside her welling up and shining out of her. But I can't.
    And then—then, afterwards, she wants something else. That's her price, to be so beautiful, to let me see how beautiful she is. She wants something else, and I can't give her that. So she punishes me. She isn't beautiful anymore. She won't let that thing in her out. She doesn't understand—she doesn't know how to make it stay. Here I've given her what she needed to be so beautiful, to be so goddamn beautiful, that's the important thing, but no, that doesn't matter, she wants something else.

She looks at me, and she isn't beautiful anymore, and she can't understand. Why I can't stay.
    You understand, Joan?

JOAN: *(A whisper)* Yes.

HASELTINE: You're sure? You're sure you want to do this?

JOAN: Yes.

HASELTINE: You think you can remember—you think you can hold on to it, after—do you think you can make it stay?
    Because I've been watching you hide it from me for three years now. I've seen it, in that instant when you look up from your work, in the moment you see me when you're coming down the stairs. I've seen how hard you've worked to keep it hidden from me.
    Can you work that hard the other way?

JOAN: *(Sad, almost angry)* If I could, I'd be beautiful forever, wouldn't I?

HASELTINE: Yes.

JOAN: *(Softly)* And if I could be beautiful forever, you'd never leave.

HASELTINE: Yes.

JOAN: You're lying to me—

HASELTINE: Maybe, then. I don't know.

JOAN: But I do. I know better. I know no matter how long—

HASELTINE: You don't know that. You don't know for sure—

JOAN: I know. You can't change.

HASELTINE: Even if I want to?

JOAN: Doesn't matter how much you want to. You can't change.

HASELTINE: Even if I'm tired? Tired of the Debbies, tired of being resourceful. Tired of it all?

JOAN: Doesn't matter how tired you are.

HASELTINE: Doesn't it?

JOAN: No.

HASELTINE: You're lying to me.

JOAN: Maybe, then.

HASELTINE: Maybe you are the woman who can make me believe I could change.

JOAN: That woman gets snapped in half. That woman gets split down the middle, after you have forgotten the wonder of finding the woman for whom you could change.
   I wish I could remember that.

(HASELTINE *and* JOAN *move toward each other.*)

(*Fade to blackout*)

Scene Three

(*Lights up on the lab, where* RUTH *is working.* THE DEBBIE *is sitting in the big easy chair. She is about thirty-five, more or less ageless looking, not pretty, dressed in a way that no one would notice, but she's not a mouse—she's a curious mix of timid self-containment.*)

(JOAN *enters the lab, and goes to her workbench without noticing* THE DEBBIE, *without looking at* RUTH. *She sits down at her workbench, begins getting out her tools.*)

JOAN: Don't say it. Don't. I deserve it. You're entitled to it. But don't. Don't even think it. Please. I know you're dying to tell me—don't pretend you're not, I know you are, but you just can't. I just can't bear to hear you say

"I told you so" till tomorrow, at the very earliest. I just can't.

RUTH: You should have called.

JOAN: I meant to.

RUTH: So I didn't worry.

JOAN: I know.

RUTH: I didn't worry, as it turns out—

JOAN: Why not?

RUTH: I had faith.

JOAN: Faith?

RUTH: That sooner or later you'd trail in and I'd get to tell you I told you so. Besides, I had plenty to do. My work, your work—

(Joan picks up the blotter on her desk.)

JOAN: Very funny. I've only got till Monday to get the Yeats letter back to the foundation, so—*(She sees there is nothing under the blotter.)* Where's the Yeats love letter I was working on! The one that's due on Monday?

RUTH: I've got it.

JOAN: Thank God, you scared me for a minute.

RUTH: It's almost done.

JOAN: You got rid of the goddamn lamination?

RUTH: Well...no. But I got rid of most of it.

(Joan looks at the work Ruth has done.)

Joan: Ruth, this is good. Really good. But what about the Whitman, you shouldn't have stopped work on your project—

RUTH: I finished that on Friday.

Joan: Look, I appreciate your help, but I've still got till Monday to get this in the mail, so—

RUTH: This is Monday, Joan.

JOAN: No it's not, it's—

RUTH: Thursday. Friday. Saturday. Sunday. Then comes Monday. That's what this is. Monday.

JOAN: That's all it is? Monday? It feels like ten years, you know, it feels like nothing, like ten minutes, and ten years, all at the same time.

What am I doing, Ruth? Am I crazy?

RUTH: Yes.

JOAN: So I'm crazy. All right. So I'm crazy. So I was crazy, and now it's over. What am I going to do now?

RUTH: You're going to turn around.

JOAN: Turn around?

(JOAN *turns around. She sees* THE DEBBIE.)

THE DEBBIE: Hello.

JOAN: Can I help you?

THE DEBBIE: No.

JOAN: Did you help her already?

RUTH: She's just waiting.

THE DEBBIE: I'm just waiting.

JOAN: For what?

THE DEBBIE: For Tom.

JOAN: Haseltine?

THE DEBBIE: Yes.

JOAN: I see. Well, that's right. That's on schedule. That's according to the great plan.

  Well, if you're waiting for Haseltine, you've come to the right place.

THE DEBBIE: Yes. She told me.

RUTH: I told her.

THE DEBBIE: I always did want to see where he worked. I've been after him to take me here. It must be wonderful, to work all day with books.

JOAN: You think so?

THE DEBBIE: Yes. And the way Tom talks about it always makes it seem that way.

JOAN: What do you work with all day?

THE DEBBIE: I teach.

JOAN: High school? Grade school?

THE DEBBIE: *(Laughing)* No, here at the University.

JOAN: You teach here?

THE DEBBIE: Yes. That's how I met Tom—it was his first day at work, he'd gotten lost and asked directions, and someone sent him to my lab instead of this one by mistake. I work in the biology department.

JOAN: Biology department?

RUTH: Is there something wrong with your hearing all of a sudden, Joan? She's a professor of biology. In the department.

THE DEBBIE: My students call me the human pipette. Not in front of me, of course.

JOAN: It's just that you don't look like a biology teacher.

RUTH: Professor, Joan.

JOAN: Or a human pipette, for that matter.

THE DEBBIE: Well, you have to see me in action. At work.

JOAN: As a matter of fact, what you do look like is a Debbie.

THE DEBBIE: Really? Then I guess I do. That's what Tom said, too. What's your name?

JOAN: Joan.

RUTH: And I'm Ruth.

THE DEBBIE: Well, it's very nice to meet you both

RUTH: Nice to meet you.

THE DEBBIE: It won't bother you two if I wait here, will it? If I watch you in action, watch you work?

RUTH: Won't bother me. Will it bother you, Joan?

JOAN: No. I don't think it will bother me to have her watch you do my work.

(An uncomfortable pause)

THE DEBBIE: Thanks.

(THE DEBBIE looks over RUTH's shoulder.)

RUTH: Here then—this is the project I just finished. It's Walt Whitman's *Leaves of Grass*. This is his own copy, first edition, and these are his revisions for the second.

THE DEBBIE: He put them on with safety pins?

RUTH: Yes.

THE DEBBIE: That looks like rust.

JOAN: It is. She's very proud of that rust.

RUTH: Is rust an animal? Is it alive?

THE DEBBIE: Well, it's mostly a reaction. I don't know if there's any way you could justify calling it an animal.

RUTH: But is it alive?

THE DEBBIE: Most things are, one way or another. If they can keep out of the way of things that are hungrier.

RUTH: Good. That helps. I already decided to keep it— but thanks.

THE DEBBIE: You're welcome. *(Another uncomfortable pause.)* Does Tom always get in to work so late?

RUTH: Hard to say. He's been on a sort of—vacation, since Thursday. So there's really no telling. Is there any telling, Joan?

JOAN: Hard to say.

RUTH: Hard to say.

THE DEBBIE: How did you both get into book conservation, if you don't mind my asking? I mean, it's fascinating to me, but how did you get interested in doing this sort of thing?

JOAN: How did you get interested in being a human pipette?

RUTH: Joan—

THE DEBBIE: Sorry. I should have realized I was bothering you.

RUTH: But you're not—

THE DEBBIE: I shouldn't ask so many questions. I'm always asking questions all the time. Which is how I got to be a human pipette, to answer yours. I was always the scrawny little kid who asked too many questions about how things worked, why things happened the way they did. People get tired of answering questions like that, after awhile. So I decided to stop asking people, and started finding out the answers for myself.

If my life were an open book, do you know what you'd find when you looked in it? Books. Books and books and more books. Books were the chief difference, between pretty girls, and smart girls, when I was growing up. Pretty girls grew up in a world of men. Smart girls grew up in a world of books. It only occurred to me, much later, that the books smart girls read are about pretty women. And that the men in those books answer all those pretty women's questions. One way or another, in the end.

JOAN: Did you come here to ask Haseltine—Tom—a question?

THE DEBBIE: Actually, yes. I did. It seemed so silly, for me to want to ask him a question, and not feel like I could, like I was not supposed to, you know? So I thought, why not. Why not just ask him.

JOAN: You think he knows the answer?

THE DEBBIE: Yes. Not only that, but I know the answer too. It's no. Oh, it will seem like yes, for awhile. It will show all the characteristic markings of yes—but in the end, it will turn out to be no.

JOAN: But if you already know the answer, why—

THE DEBBIE: I guess I can't help it—it's a habit you get into, an occupational hazard. Just because you know how something is going to turn out—just because you know, at a certain point, that the experiment is not going to be a success— *(She stops. Smiles to herself. Goes on)*—it doesn't mean you still don't have the obligation to prove it, to demonstrate it in the lab.

It's funny, to think of this being a lab when it's so different from mine. And when what you do here is so different, too.

RUTH: Because you work with living things, and we don't?

THE DEBBIE: You don't think they're alive? A little bit?

RUTH: Sometimes.

THE DEBBIE: Tom does, I think.

JOAN: Yes, he does. But they're not. They're just evidence. Artifacts. That's all they are.
Would you like to see some of his work?

RUTH: Joan!

JOAN: What he doesn't know won't hurt his work, now will it?

RUTH: He'll know, Joan.

JOAN: Come on.

(JOAN *and* THE DEBBIE *go over to* HASELTINE's *workbench. Joan removes the blotter from his work.*)

(THE DEBBIE *looks at it, excitedly.*)

THE DEBBIE: I know this—I've seen a reproduction—it's by William Blake! Oh, it's so beautiful.

JOAN: See the way the endpapers at the front have this shine, but the ones in back don't? The ones with the shine are the one's he replaced.

(THE DEBBIE *looks carefully at the page.*)

THE DEBBIE: I wouldn't have ever noticed that—

JOAN: Yes, that's the point.

RUTH: Only someone who knows what they're looking for can tell there's been a repair—and they can see Haseltine written all over it.

JOAN: Someone like you, all you see is Blake.

THE DEBBIE: *(She turns another page.)* Oh, how sad. Such a big rip, on such a beautiful page.

(Ruth comes over to look.)

THE DEBBIE: Right in the middle of the poem—you can hardly read it anymore.

JOAN: Is it the same one, Ruth?

RUTH: Eactly the same—this is how it looked when I saw it before. Joan, he could tell that we looked at. He got rid of the repair.

JOAN: How could he tell—

THE DEBBIE: Tell what? Please tell me, what's wrong?

JOAN: Nothing's wrong—exactly. Whenever we sneak a look at his work, he always knows. We put everything back exactly, but he knows.

THE DEBBIE: Looking at things does change them, you know.

RUTH: What?

THE DEBBIE: They've done tests, on the subatomic level, fired particles at a target, first when they were watching, then when they weren't. It's a little hard to believe, but the particles hit one place when someone was watching, another when they weren't.

RUTH: You mean, he really can tell when someone's been looking at his work?

THE DEBBIE: Oh, I don't think you can apply it quite like that.

JOAN: Then what do you mean?

THE DEBBIE: Just that you looked at this. You wanted to see something. And looking and wanting like that changes things.

RUTH: Maybe it was always ripped, and we imagined it—

JOAN: No. We saw it. The perfect repair.

(JOAN and RUTH begin putting everything back the way they had found it on HASELTINE's workbench.)

THE DEBBIE: (Backing away from the activity, as they continue working). Well, you all are busy—I really should go—

JOAN: What about that question you were going to ask Haseltine?

THE DEBBIE: It'll keep. It's kept this long.

JOAN: I wanted to ask you a question.

THE DEBBIE: Yes?

JOAN: I wanted to ask you a whole lot of questions. Find out all these things. Important questions—I can't remember what they were, now, but—

THE DEBBIE: Well, when you do, come ask me. I've got a class in a few minutes, so I've really got to go now, but the biology department's not that far from here. Just come to the third floor, ask for Doctor Grant. Doctor Melissa Grant. (*She is at the door.*)

JOAN: But your name is Debbie—

THE DEBBIE: No, afraid not—

JOAN: But you said—

THE DEBBIE: No, I didn't, remember? I didn't say. You said I looked like a Debbie. And I said Tom said so too.
   It was such a corny line. Such a sad line. I haven't heard a line like that since—to tell the truth, I've never heard a line like that. Not once. I guess I'm just not the kind of woman men with corny lines like that are attracted to. So it was sort of a treat, for me. When he said it. He said, "You look like a Debbie."And he looked so sad. So lost. Actually, he really was lost, but still. He said, "You look like a Debbie." (*She almost starts to cry.*) And I wanted so bad to say "yes". (*She is gone.*)

JOAN: I didn't think they'd be so nice.

RUTH: She was, wasn't she.

JOAN: I liked her right away.

RUTH: Is that why you were so nasty to her at first?

JOAN: Yes. I didn't want her to be nice. I wanted her to be horrible.

RUTH: So, since she wasn't, you were?

JOAN: Something like that. She wasn't really a Debbie, you know.

RUTH: Yes she was.

JOAN: She was a fake, a counterfeit. A forged Debbie.

RUTH: Like you?

JOAN: No. Not anymore.

RUTH: What was it like?

JOAN: Being a Debbie?

RUTH: Yeah.

JOAN: Easy. At first. Like falling off a log. It seemed like the most natural thing in the world to be. And then it turned into the hardest thing on earth.
  He was eating these hot dogs.

(Lights up on HASELTINE, wearing his jacket and with his cap on, climbing the stairs, holding a brown paper sack. He reaches into the sack, and pulls out a package of hot dogs.)

JOAN: We'd gone out to get something to eat, and he couldn't even wait till we got back. He just ripped them open, and started eating.

(HASELTINE opens the package of hot dogs with his teeth, takes out a hot dog, begins eating.)

JOAN: And I couldn't make myself climb the stairs. I couldn't make myself put one foot—then the other—it was impossible, Ruth— *(She lies down at the bottom of the stairs, splayed out, as if she has just fallen down them.)* Even to think about climbing those stairs.

HASELTINE: *(Turns, sees her lying there)* Get up. They'll think you're dead.

JOAN: I am dead. *(To RUTH)* And the thing is, Ruth, I really didn't think it would feel like this. I really didn't. *(To HASELTINE)* You know, I didn't think it would feel like this. I really didn't. I didn't think it would feel so... so....

HASELTINE/JOAN: So...so...so...

(HASELTINE gestures, waving the hot dog in the air, as if to be saying, "Come on, come on".)

JOAN: ...appropriate.

(JOAN *catches sight of* HASELTINE *swallowing a huge section of hot dog.*)

JOAN: *(To* HASELTINE:*)* You eat funny. You eat late at night, you cram the food into your mouth, you run from room to room swallowing, you don't let me see your face.

HASELTINE: I let you see my face. *(He goes on eating.)*

JOAN: *(To* RUTH*)* I looked at him. Eating and eating. Eating and eating, and he never gets enough. *(To* HASELTINE:*)* What does it feel like when I say things like that to you?

HASELTINE: *(Shrugs)* You know.

JOAN: I know, but tell me anyway. Console me. Humor me. Honor your dead. Tell me what you think when I say things like that.

HASELTINE: Not much.
  That you're a woman. Like the rest.

JOAN: And I can't help saying them, is that it?

HASELTINE: Something like that.
  Maybe you're just tired.

JOAN: Dead tired.

HASELTINE: Something like that.

JOAN: Actually, I love the way you eat. It's very endearing. *(To* RUTH*)* I hate myself, of course, for liking it. I know I shouldn't. I was brought up to be horrified by a man eating the way he does. *(To* HASELTINE:*)* I was brought up to be horrified by everything about you. Starting at the top. And working its way down. Every part of you.

HASELTINE: Usually you don't talk like this.

JOAN: Like the Debbies?

HASELTINE: Whatever.

JOAN: That's because I wasn't dead before.

HASELTINE: You're not dead.

JOAN: How does it make you feel, come on, really. To listen to me talk like I'm a Debbie.

HASELTINE: Hungry.

JOAN: You were hungry before.

HASELTINE: So. I'm hungry now.
  Come on, Joan. Don't be mad. We had a good time. We had a good, long laugh. We needed that.

JOAN: I'll never see you eat again, now that I'm dead. It makes me very sad.

HASELTINE: You're not dead.

JOAN: And you're not hungry.

HASELTINE: I look hungry. I feel hungry. I'm eating like I'm hungry.

JOAN: Yes, yes. But you're not.

HASELTINE: Do I look hungry?

JOAN: Yes.

HASELTINE: Am I eating like I'm hungry?

JOAN: Oh, yes.

HASELTINE: Seems to me the evidence is in my favor. Seems to me.

JOAN: Oh, yes, it seems that way. But it's just an act. You have an excellent hungry act. You've got it down.

HASELTINE: Why would I eat if I weren't hungry?

JOAN: Maybe you're hungry because you eat.

HASELTINE: If I didn't eat, I'd be dead.

JOAN: Maybe you are dead, and you're eating to try to fool yourself. Maybe you're—

HASELTINE: This is a stupid conversation.

JOAN: *(To* RUTH*)* And believe me, it was. The kind of stupid conversation you can have only when you think the other person in the room is the one person who knows you better than anybodyin the world—but it turns out he doesn't even recognize you.

HASELTINE: Baby, don't be mad at me.

JOAN: You don't even recognize yourself. I mean, you appear to be lying at the bottom of the stairs—but you're really in a car, going a hundred miles an hour headed straight for a cliff; you're in a plummeting 747, in a tailspin or a nose-dive, it doesn't matter which; you're on top of the Empire State Building, when the freak winds gust too fast—and inside you this voice is screaming *pull the rip cord it's right there, everything's going to be all right* and you scream back *what rip cord* and the voice says that one there—*that man beside you— grab a hold of him, hold on tight—a man like that could jump from the moon to the earth and it would be all right!* Because that's the way he made you feel. That you could jump off the moon, with him, and land safely on earth. Gravity wouldn't stand a chance against that man. When he held you tight.

HASELTINE: Come on, Joan. What are we getting all upset about here, anyway? A fucking package of hot dogs?

JOAN: *We are not talking about hot dogs!!!*

HASELTINE: We're not?

JOAN: *Why would we be talking about hot dogs at a time like this! You know we are not talking about hot dogs!*

RUTH: *(Pause)* He was really talking about hot dogs, wasn't he?

HASELTINE: Eight fucking hot dogs...

JOAN: Yeah. He was. I was lying there dead, destroyed over a man who was really talking about hot dogs.

HASELTINE: Come on, baby, get up from there.

JOAN: No.

HASELTINE: You gonna spend the whole night lying there?

JOAN: Maybe.

HASELTINE: Why?

JOAN: Because, as it turns out, I appear to have been looking my whole life to find a man I could lie here talking about hot dogs with.

HASELTINE: You're talking crazy.

JOAN: Believe me. The revelation of this moment as my life's ambition comes as much of a surprise to me as it does to you.
   God, I had such plans. Such hopes. Such stupid little dreams of the accident of happiness.

JOAN/RUTH: Happiness. Happiness. Happiness.

HASELTINE: You want me to say I'm sorry?

Okay. *(He shrugs.)* I'm sorry.

JOAN: For what.

HASELTINE: You know.

JOAN: *For what.*

HASELTINE: For doing...that.

JOAN: What.

HASELTINE: For...

JOAN: For treating me like a Debbie.

HASELTINE: You wanted that, Joan.

JOAN: No. That was a mistake. *(To RUTH)* It was an accident. But the problem with accidents is, it's hard to tell where an accident begins. Does it start inside you, or in the thing that hits you?

HASELTINE: You said, look at me. Look at me, and I'll be beautiful forever. Remember, Joan? You said—

Joan: No. That was someone else. Someone very brave. Or very stupid. *(She gets up and walks away from* HASELTINE.*)* Well, I'm not either.

HASELTINE: What do you want from me, Joan? You want me to say I'm sorry you looked so beautiful?

*(*HASELTINE *calls after* JOAN *as she walks away.)*

HASELTINE: Is that really what you want from me, Joan? *(Lights begin to fade on Haseltine.)*

*(*JOAN *is back in the lab with* RUTH.*)*

JOAN: *(She picks up a dart.)* Men. *(She throws a dart.)*

HASELTINE: *(To the empty air)* Well, I won't. I won't say I'm sorry. I saw it. You wanted me to look at you, and see how beautiful you were. You wanted this, Joan! And for one instant—

JOAN: Men. *(She throws another dart.)*

HASELTINE: —for one instant—you were the most beautiful woman in the world.

(Lights down on Haseltine.)

JOAN: Men. *(She starts to throw a dart, then doesn't.)* Men. Men! This doesn't work anymore.

RUTH: Sure it does, you're just out of practice.

JOAN: And practice makes perfect?

RUTH: Sometimes.

JOAN: No. Practice never makes perfect. Perfect is an accident. Except here, in the lab, where perfect is worse than an accident. It's just plain fogery, when you do something perfect here.

RUTH: You gonna be all right?

Joan: Yes. *(Dart)* No. *(Dart)* I guess so. *(Dart. She goes to the board, pulls out the darts, and puts them down.)*

RUTH: You want to take over on the Yeats letter? Take your mind off it?

Joan: A Yeats love letter is not eactly the thing to take my mind off it.

(Lights up on HASELTINE, *at a lecturn.)*

HASELTINE: Once the words are gone, you can't fill them in again.

JOAN: You go ahead and finish it up, Ruth. I'll just go on back home. *(*JOAN *starts to leave.)*

HASELTINE: Sometimes you drop a page into solution, to bathe it, to clear it, and the words float away before your eyes. Sometimes they fade, just from the action of sunlight, evaporating into the air. Sometimes, it is just the moment of seeing, the very act of reading, that wears them away.

Joan: *(Turning back to* RUTH*)* Ruth?

Ruth: What?

JOAN: If you're still burning up to tell me I told you so, you could stop by tonight, and tell me.

RUTH: Joan— *(She holds out her arms, and hugs* JOAN *tight.)* Of course I will.

*(*JOAN *starts to cry.* RUTH *holds her.)*

HASELTINE: All around you, you see the words fading, but the rules say: This is not a tragedy. The rules say: This is the price. This is what happens to paper and print in our hands.

(Lights fade on the lab.)

HASELTINE: This is the nature of things: To become warn and bruised and frayed. Only something new has the right to perfection of surface, only the untouched

has that unmarred finish, that soft, bright shine. Marks
and scars are the evidence, they are the truth of the
journey of any object that lives its life in our hands.
And only a criminal would seek to erase this evidence.
Only a criminal—or a fool—would be blind to the
beauty of time.

But you never feel like a criminal, at the moment you
make the perfect repair. You feel like a hero. Because at
that moment you remember that heroes always break
the rules, too.

(Lights up on JOAN *at the bottom of the tallest stairway.)*

JOAN: I climbed the stairs.

HASELTINE: Just this once, you tell yourself. Just this
one time will be enough for me. I am not a criminal,
just—this—once, let me feel what perfection is. Let me
be the hero, and make something beautiful forever, this
one time.

JOAN: I climbed the stairs, and he was there. He was
there, and I walked through him into another world
and everything that was ever ugly about me dropped
away from me like water. I was free of it all.

HASELTINE: And it feels...perfection feels...for just a
moment...but then it's gone. It can't change you. And
this is what makes you a criminal.

JOAN: I climbed the stairs, and he was there, and he
freed me from ugliness forever. And the longing
bucked inside me. And the heat kicked in. The heat
which does not lie kicked in and in.

HASELTINE: Perfection burns in your hands one
moment, but the next it's gone and to get it back, you
will break every rule, you will pay any price. But it
doesn't matter what you pay. You are holding on to a
moment you cannot hold on to. You open your hands

and there is only empty air. Again, and again, and
again.

JOAN: I climbed the stairs. And he was there. And the
heat kicked in and in. And I was beautiful—almost—
forever. Almost. Forever. And nothing changed.

HASELTINE: I found out, too late. You must do the
work, and you must follow the rules, and you must
never dream of perfection. Because if perfection cannot
change you, you are doomed to chase after it forever.
Perfection. That never stays.

(Lights fade on HASELTINE.*)*

JOAN: He was this bright shiny thing, that fell into
my lap one day, like Jove on a holiday. His face fairly
burned when he looked at a woman, any woman. His
face lit up the sky. And I thought, if any man can see
me, and make me beautiful, he's the one.

   I climb the stairs, and I think—beauty is just a kind of
accident too. I climb the stairs, and I think—happiness
is different than a dream. I climb the stairs, and I think,
where did I get these ideas, why am I making it so
hard on myself, why am I dragging this heavy weight
up the stairs? I climb the stairs. And I know he's not
there. *(She is at the landing to her apartment. She looks
up, to the the top of the stairway, then opens the door to her
apartment.)*

(Lights fade to blackout.)

END OF PLAY

www.ingramcontent.com/pod-product-compliance
Lightning Source LLC
Chambersburg PA
CBHW052204090426
42741CB00010B/2400